T0060974

African American Religion:
A Very Short Introduction

VERY SHORT INTRODUCTIONS are for anyone wanting a stimulating and accessible way in to a new subject. They are written by experts and have been translated into more than 40 different languages.

The series began in 1995 and now covers a wide variety of topics in every discipline. The VSI library now contains nearly 400 volumes—a Very Short Introduction to everything from Indian philosophy to psychology and American History—and continues to grow in every subject area.

Very Short Introductions available now:

Available soon:

For more information visit our website
www.oup.com/vsi/

Eddie S. Glaude Jr.

AFRICAN
AMERICAN
RELIGION

A Very Short Introduction

OXFORD
UNIVERSITY PRESS

OXFORD

UNIVERSITY PRESS

Oxford University Press is a department of the
University of Oxford. It furthers the University's objective
of excellence in research, scholarship, and education
by publishing worldwide.

Oxford   New York

Auckland   Cape Town   Dar es Salaam   Hong Kong   Karachi
Kuala Lumpur   Madrid   Melbourne   Mexico City   Nairobi
New Delhi   Shanghai   Taipei   Toronto

With offices in

Argentina   Austria   Brazil   Chile   Czech Republic   France   Greece
Guatemala   Hungary   Italy   Japan   Poland   Portugal   Singapore
South Korea   Switzerland   Thailand   Turkey   Ukraine   Vietnam

Oxford is a registered trade mark of Oxford University Press
in the UK and certain other countries.

Published in the United States of America by
Oxford University Press
198 Madison Avenue, New York, NY 10016

Library of Congress Cataloging-in-Publication Data
Glaude, Eddie S., Jr., 1968–
African American Religion : A Very Short Introduction / Eddie S. Glaude Jr.
pages   cm. — (Very short introductions)
Includes bibliographical references and index.
ISBN 978-0-19-518289-7 (paperback)
1. African Americans—Religion.   I. Title.
BR563.N4G59 2014
200.89'96073—dc23
2014007043

Printed by Integrated Books International, United States of America

To Albert Jordy Raboteau

Contents

List of illustrations

Acknowledgments

I am extremely grateful to my colleague Imani Perry.
She read each chapter twice and listened patiently to my
handwringing about what to include and exclude in the
book. I also want to thank Josef Sorett. Josef read the book
in its early stages and offered tracked comments that were
tremendously helpful in clarifying my overall approach. Melvin
Rogers did the same and was particularly helpful in pushing me to
clarify my pragmatic framework. I also owe a great debt to
Jonathan Walton. Our conversations and his reading of the
manuscript helped me complete what turned out to be a
challenging task. The mistakes are mine alone, but the
generosity of my friends is evident throughout the book. Kijan
Bloomfield Maxam has also been a true blessing. Kijan is a
graduate student in Princeton's religion department; she hunted
down images, read chapters, and suggested further readings.
We have come a long way together since her undergraduate days
at Bowdoin College.

Thanks to my family, Winnifred Brown-Glaude and Langston
Glaude, for enduring my absences as I struggled with the demand
for brevity and the mountain of material before me. Langston
refers to my home office as the cave. I pray that I have not been
pondering shadows.

Finally, I want to thank Professor Albert Raboteau. I consider myself his student, and I have been blessed to call him a colleague. The breath of his spirit and the power of his intellect have opened pathways for so many to travel. This Very Short Introduction, with its flaws and obvious personal prejudices, is a tribute to him and what he has done to help create and sustain this wonderful field of study. Al helped me see more clearly the insight of Howard Thurman: that "we are not dealing with a conceptual approach to religion but with an intensely practical one based on the tragedy of great need." I hope that I have captured some piece of this insight in what follows.

Chapter 1

The category of "African American religion"

I grew up Catholic on the coast of Mississippi. It is an old black Catholic community, one rooted in the Josephite tradition. The Josephite Society of the Sacred Heart was formed in 1871. Its mission was to serve black freedmen and women in the aftermath of the Civil War "through the proclamation of the Gospel and personal witness." They established a presence on the coast of Mississippi in 1907 with the founding of St. Peter the Apostle Parish in Pascagoula. My father's family belonged to this church. Generations of Glaudes were christened here, took their first communion, and received confirmation. We were part of the roughly 1.2 million black Catholics in the United States.

The Catholic church I grew up in was radically different from my grandmother's. Mine bore the effects of Vatican II and conducted its ministry in a post–Jim Crow world (although the "white" Catholic church still existed across town). No more liturgies in Latin, our priest often wore Kente cloth, and we had a gospel choir. My mother, along with her friends in the choir, would sing, "Soon and very soon we are going to see the King." They would rhythmically sway back and forth, and give God the glory in praise song while the members of St. Peter's sat quietly with a slight rock of the shoulders and a reserved pat of the foot that kept time. Our church choir was even invited to a local gospel festival. Choirs

1. In 1836, a small order of nuns (later known as the Sisters of the Holy Family) was founded in New Orleans. This was one of many Catholic organizations recognized by the Catholic Church along the Gulf Coast in the second half of the nineteenth century dedicated to educating slaves and serving the poor and elderly.

from churches all over our little town gathered to sing and worship. This was my first experience of black Pentecostal and Baptist traditions.

I sat at the far left corner of the pew in a stereotypically small southern church house. The seat was available only because we arrived early. The church was packed. It was hot. Mississippi heat has a way of sticking to you; it slows the pace of life but adds a level of intensity to any activity. The room was thick with sweat and anticipation. An older, heavy-set woman sat next to me. She wore a bright floral-print dress, and her hair was freshly pressed (I could smell the effects of the hot comb). Beads of sweat trickled down the side of her face.

"Scoot down a bit, baby," she said.

I moved as far as I could, but there wasn't much room. As the preacher began to say a few words before offering prayer, I sat in amazement. He was a poet and, unlike Father Veal, who was so mind-numbingly deliberate in everything he said, this man made the Gospel come alive.

The preacher started to pray. No one stood. Everyone bowed his or her head. I heard something strange and incredible. He started slowly. The congregation murmured in agreement. His pace quickened. His words began to take on a rhythm, and the folk began to shout back: "Amen" "Yes, Lord" "Yes, Jesus." The woman next to me rocked back and forth, bumping against me as she called back to the preacher. I had never heard or seen anything like this. St. Peter's, on the other hand, was quiet, the priest spoke in hushed tones. But this preacher prayed with more intensity. As he ended, everyone seemed on edge and emotions threatened to burst open the church. Then the unique sound of a Hammond organ took over, and one of the choirs marched in clapping their hands and singing at the tops of their lungs. This was true theater. The music took my breath away.

Women with the phrasing of Sarah Vaughan and the sound of Bessie Smith sang "On Calvary," and men who could give B. B. King and Sam Cooke a run for their money crooned "I Don't Feel No Ways Tired." The small church literally rocked as choirs and the congregation shouted and praised. I sat with my mouth agape, when suddenly the woman next to me began to speak in a loud whisper. She started to shake, waving her right hand in the air, saying, "Thank you, Jesus! Thank you, Jesus! Thank you, Jesus." I sat next to her in horror as she fell back in the pew and onto me. She had "caught the spirit." This is what W. E. B. Du Bois, the noted African American intellectual, referred to as "the pythian madness, a demoniac possession that lent terrible reality to song and word." And like Du Bois, such an experience was completely foreign to me and yet wholly familiar.

Here, in this little house of worship on the coast of Mississippi, I experienced what Du Bois described in *The Souls of Black Folk* (1903) as the three things that characterized the religion of the slave: the preacher, the music, and the frenzy. For him, each one of these accounts for the distinctiveness of black religious life and sets the stage for the importance of "the Negro church" as a civic institution in African American life more generally. The preacher is the paradigmatic figure for black leaders; the music offers a glimpse into the blues-soaked soul of a people—it is their plaintive cry under the storm and stress of American life. The frenzy (the shouting), for Du Bois, captures that delicate balance between joy and terror that shadows black life in the United States. It is the eruption of the spirit in ordinary time that assures the presence of God amid the absurdity of white supremacy.

All three features are powerfully expressed in what Du Bois called "the Negro church." This institution stood at the epicenter of black life. Voluntary associations that addressed the social and economic needs of the community formed within its walls. Church buildings provided the physical space for the education of children. They also offered space for political debate and organizing. Here one acquired a sense of the religious worldview of a captured people, for "the Negro church," under the brutal weight of slavery and Jim Crow, gave its members and its community languages to imagine themselves apart from the dehumanizing practices of white supremacy. One hears this in the plaintive sound of slave spirituals:

> Canaan land is the land for me,
> And let God's saints come in.
> There was a wicked man,
> He kept them children in Egypt land.
> Canaan land is the land for me,
> And let God's saints come in.

Or, in the moving words of modern gospel music:

I don't feel no ways tired,
I've come too far from where I started from.
Nobody told me that the road would be easy,
I don't believe He brought me this far to leave me.

Each song envisions the possibility of a brighter future predicated on an abiding faith in God, an insight gained in communion and worship with others.

But to think of the preacher, the music, and the frenzy or, more generally, "the Negro or black church," as definitive of *all* of African American religious life denies the religious differences and complexity within black communities. Not all African Americans are Christian nor are they specifically Protestant. American soil has always been and remains fertile ground for a plurality of religious views and practices. Black religious life is no different. Black Christians, Muslims, Jews, practitioners of conjure, voodoo, Yoruba, or other traditional African religions all flourish in black communities throughout the United States. Of course, black Protestantism remains dominant: 83 percent of African Americans self-identify as Christian, and of that number 78 percent are Protestant (only 5 percent are Roman Catholic). But, we must recognize the differences even within black Protestantism (different black denominational histories, Pentecostalism, non-denominationalism). If we are to fully understand African American religious life in the United States, we must also take into account the 12 percent who identify as Christian but are unaffiliated with any particular group.

A subtle distinction must be made here. *African American religious life* consists in all the varied religious practices that occur within black communities. Those practices range from people who attend traditional mainline black churches (like African Methodist Episcopal churches and black Baptist churches), and charismatic churches to those who are Muslim to African Americans who practice Buddhism—just to name a few. Scholars offer sociological accounts of these different groupings. Theologians explain the various doctrines of some of them, and religious historians tell us how they came into existence. But it would be a mistake to say that all these different groups are examples of *African American religion*. African American religion, in my view, sets apart something more specific.

A pragmatic approach to African American religion

What is African American religion? An informative body of literature has been written about the difficulties in the study of religion generally. Many of the concerns evidenced in these conversations (debates about whether religion is reducible to some other more fundamental notion) are interestingly complicated when we think about religion in tandem with race. Or, more specifically, the issue becomes even messier when the modifier "black" or "African American" describes religion. These adjectives bear the unusual burden of a difficult history that colors the way religion is practiced and understood in the United States. They register the horror of slavery and the terror of Jim Crow as well as the richly textured experiences of a captured people, for whom sorrow stands alongside joy. It is in this context, one characterized by the ever-present need to account for one's presence in the world in the face of white supremacy, that African American religion takes on such significance.

African American religious life is not reducible to those wounds. That life contains within it avenues for solace and comfort in God, answers to questions about who we take ourselves to be and about our relation to the mysteries of the universe; moreover, meaning is found, for some, in submission to God, in obedience to creed and dogma, and in ritual practice. Here evil is accounted for. And hope, at least for some, is assured. In short, African American religious life is as rich and as complicated as the religious life of other groups in the United States, but African American religion emerges in the encounter between faith, in all of its complexity, and white supremacy.

My approach assumes that the political and social context in the United States is a necessary though not sufficient condition of any study of something called African American religion. If the phrase "African American religion" is to have any descriptive usefulness at all, it must signify something *more* than African Americans who are religious. In fact, African Americans practice a number of different religions. There are black people who are Buddhist, Jehovah Witness, Mormon, and Baha'i. But that African Americans practice these traditions does not lead us to describe them as black Buddhism or black Mormonism. African American religion singles out something more substantive than that. This something *more* does not have to be an idea of religion, which stands apart from social and historical forces that impinge on the lives of African Americans. Nor does it refer to a definite kind of experience that is itself religious or a religious consciousness as distinct from other forms of consciousness. My aim here is not to secure the unique status of the category of African American religion "as of its own kind."

The adjective refers instead to a racial context within which religious meanings have been produced and reproduced (I will defer consideration of how religion has also produced particular racial meanings). The history of slavery and racial discrimination in the United States birthed particular religious formations among African Americans. African Americans converted to Christianity, for example, in the context of slavery. Many left predominantly white denominations to form their own after experiencing racial proscription and in pursuit of a sense of self-determination. Some embraced a distinctive interpretation of Islam to make sense of their condition in the United States. Given that history, we can reasonably and accurately describe certain variants of Christianity and Islam as African American and mean something beyond the rather uninteresting claim that black individuals belong to these different religious traditions.

7

Of course, African American religious practices can be understood apart from the social and political context that, in some ways, called them into being. And there are numerous studies that do just that. Attention to context, however, helps to explain why the scholar has called the particular religious formation "African American religion." In other words, African American religion is the invention of scholars who, with particular aims and purposes, seek to describe, analyze, and theorize the religious practices of African Americans under a particular racial regime.

The words "black" or "African American" work as markers of difference: as a way of signifying a tradition of struggle against white supremacist practices and a cultural repertoire that reflects that unique journey as evidenced in religious meanings produced under certain conditions. The phrase calls up a particular history and culture in our efforts to understand the religious practices of a particular people. When I use the phrase "African American religion" then, I am not referring to something that can be defined substantively apart from the thicket of varied practices; rather, my aim is to orient you in a particular way to the material under consideration, to call attention to a sociopolitical history that informs the topic at hand, and to single out the workings of the human imagination and spirit under particular conditions.

Sentences that begin, "African American religion is…" are rarely simply descriptive. They typically convey certain normative assumptions about what that religion is, has been, and ought to be, like "African American religion is prophetic" or "African American religion is emotional." But to understand the sentence "African American religion is…" only in this way risks the problem of reifying a particular understanding of black religious practices (of denying complexity, ambiguity, and contradiction by snatching varied practices out of the messiness of history). It is much better to understand such utterances as a *procedure of differentiation and invocation*: as a way of saying that you ought

8

to give more attention to *this* as opposed to *that*, and a recollection of history that makes that distinction worthwhile.

When Howard Thurman, the great twentieth-century black theologian, declared that the slave dared to redeem the religion profaned in his midst, he offered a particular understanding of black Christianity: this expression of Christianity was not the idolatrous embrace of Christian doctrine that justified the superiority of white people and the subordination of black people. Instead, black Christianity embraced the liberating power of Jesus's example: his sense that all, no matter their station in life, were children of God. Thurman sought to orient the reader to a specific inflection of Christianity in the hands of those who lived as slaves. For him and for me, that difference made a difference. We need only listen to the spirituals, give attention to the way African Americans interpreted the Gospel, and to how they invoked Jesus in their lives. This approach brings into view the particular circumstances that cast Christianity in *this* way as opposed to *that*.

We can also think about this in terms of the negative sentence "This isn't African American religion," or the more familiar claim "This isn't 'black church.'" Such sentences say more about the commitments of the person who utters them than about actual religious practices. What is being noted here is the absence of some *thing*, that some essential element of what constitutes African American Christianity is missing. If we think pragmatically, such utterances point us in a particular direction in relation to the practices under consideration. They call our attention to the absence of cultural markers that have historically attached themselves to African Americans (a certain style of worship for example) or the failure to make explicit connections to African American life or to the politics of the person who utters the claim. So, these sentences also do the work of differentiation and invocation. They draw attention to what makes us "us" as opposed to "them," and that distinction involves attention to "this" as opposed to "that." What should be of interest is not the matter of essential ideas of "us" and "them," but rather the content of "this" and "that" and how that content changes our understanding of the object under consideration.

We cannot deny that African American religious life has developed, for much of its history, under captured conditions. The esteemed historian of religion Charles Long is right to insist on the centrality of the importance of what he calls "the involuntary presence of the black community in America" as a distinctive methodological concern for African American religion. Slaves had to forge lives amid the brutal reality of their condition and imagine possibilities beyond their status as slaves. Religion offered a powerful resource in their efforts. They imagined possibilities beyond anything their circumstances suggested. As religious bricoleurs, they created, as did their children and children's children, on the level of religious consciousness, and that creativity gave African American religion its distinctive hue and timber.

African Americans drew on the cultural knowledge, however fleeting, of their African past. They selected what they found compelling and rejected what they found unacceptable in the traditions of white slaveholders. In some cases, they reached for traditions outside of the United States altogether. They took the bits and pieces of their complicated lives, the received knowledge and the newly experienced insight, and created distinctive expressions of the general order of existence that anchored their efforts to live amid the pressing nastiness of life. They created what scholars call African American religion.

Three examples: Conjure, Christianity, and Islam

Any study of African American religion must begin with the claim that the particular and dynamic circumstances of African American life constituted the soil for black religious imaginings.

Those imaginings ranged from belief in God and her active role in history (that is, a distinctive theological voice) to an insistence that all is not settled, which provided the opening for imaginative leaps beyond the immediate horrors of life. One can witness and hear the distinctiveness of African Americans in the sermonic style of black preaching in churches or in the temples/mosques of the Nation of Islam or in the glorious sounds of black religious music and in worship services throughout the United States. This cultural imprint gives African American religion its unique quality. I am not denying here the importance of African Americans in predominantly white denominations (about 15 percent of African Americans are members of evangelical dominations like the Assemblies of God, and 4 percent are in mainline denominations like the Disciples of Christ) or any of the varied expressions of black religiosity in American life. There is simply a difference between the religions African Americans practice and African American religion. That difference resides in the way history, social, and political context inform and shape the very substance of religious expression.

Three key ideas organize my approach to the study of African American religion. First, I view African American religion as a *practice of freedom*. Here black religious imagination is used in the service of opening up spaces closed down by white supremacy. The political nature of that opening varies. It is not necessarily progressive or conservative. Rather, religion becomes the site for self-creation and for communal advancement with political implication. This view requires situating African American religion within the broader dynamic of African American history. Second, I understand African American religion as a *sign of difference*. The phrase differentiates particular religious practices from others by reference to specific historical and social contexts that give them shape. African American religion explicitly rejects, as best as possible, the idolatry of white supremacy by proclaiming itself, in practice, as different. And, third, my approach to African American religion insists on its *open-ended orientation*. African

American religion offers resources for African Americans to imagine themselves beyond the constraints of now. This belief that "all is not settled," rooted in God's grace and the evidence of history, enables broad leaps of faith that deepen aspirational claims for freedom.

Taken together, these three elements help us navigate the complex religious history of African Americans in the United States. They also anchor the kinds of stories we write that say something specific about what it might mean to be black and to hold religious views in a country that is simultaneously democratic, predominantly Christian, and racist. The history of African American religion demands that we give attention to a thick political and social history in the United States. Each chapter in this book introduces its topic within the context of its historical moment and the particular ways in which race and racism affect black life generally.

I have chosen three representative examples of African American religion. Each demonstrates how African American religion can be seen as a practice of freedom, a sign of difference, and as an open-ended mode of living religiously. Conjure, for example, draws our attention to the continuity and discontinuity with African religious practices as well as a particular instance of a religious imagination, which differentiates itself from those who enslaved and discriminated against others. It shows how the debates in the field of religious studies about the difference between magic and religion fall apart when an oppressed people take up secret religious knowledge to make sense of their lives. Beginning with conjure also disrupts the view that black Christianity constitutes the totality of African American religion. Here we see a religious practice that connects with a distant past, shadows Christian practice, and animates everyday life in ways that offer some semblance of control over circumstances that seem, at first glance, uncontrollable.

Even though we began with conjure, black Christianity makes up the bulk of this treatment of African American religion for obvious reasons. The majority of African Americans, even today, are Christian. More importantly, black Christianity has played a critical role in the history of African American responses to white supremacy in the United States. Four chapters examine this complex history. Each introduces key moments and personalities, as well as the importance of black churches over the course of three historical periods: an early phase (1760–1863); a modern phase (1863–1980); and a contemporary phase (1980 to the present).

Of course, there is always something somewhat arbitrary about periodization. The beginning and cut-off dates represent an attempt to impose some semblance of order on a very messy terrain. In this instance, the three phases of black Christianity help track the extraordinary shifts in the material conditions of black life that affect the form and content of black Christian expression in the United States. They reflect my insistence on the centrality of the social and political context for the study of African American religion.

The periodization also keeps in the foreground the dynamism of American racism: that what racial proscription looked like in the early nineteenth century is dramatically different from what we see in the twenty-first century. The early phase extends from the Revolutionary era to the emergence of the modern American nation-state during the Civil War. It covers the period when the economy of slavery dominated political matters up to the Emancipation Proclamation and the end of the plantation regime. Here black Christianity resided, for the most part, in the shadows of plantation life as an "invisible institution," and in the North began to take institutional form in independent denominations particularly concerned with the scourge of slavery. The presence/absence of slavery defined the contours, even among free black populations, of black Christianity during this period.

The modern phase represents the period of the nationalization of black Christianity, as the "invisible institution" of the slaveholding

South became visible and as black denominations in the North extended their missions overtly into the South. The effects of industrialization and modernization also marked this phase. Cities emerged as the central trope of American life. Moreover, massive numbers of African Americans migrated from southern rural towns to cities in the South, the North, and the West. The new migrants changed the demographics of American cities as they confronted new forms of labor discipline and different social constraints. The modern phase is also characterized by American imperial ambition and the consolidation of a new racial regime called Jim Crow. Racial segregation and the extralegal violence that attended its implementation fundamentally shaped the expression of black Christianity during this period. In fact, the historic relationship between African American Christianity and black politics is made even more explicit with the civil rights movement and its clear ties to black Christian life.

The contemporary phase begins with the election of Ronald Reagan in 1980 and the changing landscape of American Christianity. Reagan's election was a victory for a certain conception of government and economics, one that would fundamentally reconceive how the nation imagined the public good. His election also signaled the return of forces deeply skeptical about the gains of the black freedom struggle of the twentieth century. Ironically, appeals to color blindness served as a justification for rolling back civil rights legislation. It is also a period characterized by the effects of deindustrialization unleashed in the 1970s with the media mogul Henry Luce's wildly optimistic claim that the so-called American Century ended in 1972 with the OPEC crisis, the loss of the manufacturing sector with the ascendance of a finance- and service-based economy, and the saturation of popular cultural forms across all domains of American life. In short, the Age of Reagan, as some scholars call it, represents a moment of rapid decline for certain segments of black America. And it certainly serves as context for transformations in the form and content of black Christianity with the ascendance of megachurches (churches with more than two thousand people) and a deracialized "prosperity gospel" (in which wealth is a sign of God's favor irrespective of persistent racial inequality).

Although race continues to animate much of American society, the ability to talk about the subject has been greatly curtailed by the prominence of appeals to color blindness and idealistic claims that with the election of our first African American president, race does not matter in the same way that it did in the mid-twentieth century. Indeed, the allure of a postracial society complicates the continued relevance of African American religion.

Finally, I turn to African American Islam. In some ways, Islam best represents the idea of African American religion as a practice of freedom and a sign of difference. For those African Americans who embraced Islam during the modern phase, their conversion was as much an expression of skepticism about Christianity and the United States as it was an acceptance of Islam. I also situate African American Islam within a broader global religious imagination that seeks to expand how African Americans understand themselves as members of a global community, an understanding that has shifted and morphed in light of the pressures of Muslim immigration to the United States. Those pressures have involved, among other things, an insistence on decoupling Islam from the particulars of African American racial experience.

Each example brings into view the various ways African Americans have made sense, with religious tools, of a world that all too often declares them inferior—a world that all too often relegates them to the shadows. The preacher, the frenzy, and the music (what I experienced in that small church house on the coast of Mississippi) stand as just one dimension of a complex religious response that has made possible freedom dreams, that has rejected the evil of white supremacy, and has insisted that the future remains open. The phrase "African American religion" turns our attention to this wonderfully human response to the ordeal of living.

Chapter 2
Conjure and African American religion

In 1845, Frederick Douglass, perhaps the most famous slave in American history, published his first autobiography. He eventually wrote three versions of his life story. Each chronicled the brutality of slavery and his relentless pursuit of freedom. In all three versions, the battle with Edward Covey, the slaveholder charged to break Douglass, stands as a transformative moment.

> Long before daylight, I was called to go and rub, curry and feed, the horses. I obeyed, and was glad to obey. But whilst thus engaged, whilst in the act of throwing down some blades from the loft, Mr. Covey entered the stable with a long rope; and just as I was half out of the loft, he caught hold of my legs and was about tying me. As soon as I found what he was up to, I gave a sudden spring, and as I did so, he holding to my legs, I was brought sprawling on the stable floor. Mr. Covey seemed now to think he had me, and could do what he pleased; but at this moment—*from whence came the spirit I don't know*—I resolved to fight; and, suiting my action to the resolution, I seized Covey hard by the throat; and as I did so, I rose.

As Douglass wrote, "This battle with Mr. Covey was the turning point in my career as a slave. It rekindled the few expiring embers of freedom, and revived within me a sense of my own manhood." It was a conversion moment of sorts, sparked by a sudden, even desperate, willingness to risk his life. Just a few pages earlier in the autobiography Douglass recounted how Covey had transformed him into a brute; how "the dark night of slavery closed in upon me."

Douglass resisted the violence of slavery, and he did so within the context of a scene wrought with complex religious meanings and sensibilities. He was not shy about exposing the religious hypocrisy of slaveholders. Covey was a leading member of his Methodist church, and Master Auld, Douglass's owner, was also an ardent Christian. Douglass wrote, "Were I to be again reduced to the chains of slavery next to the enslavement, I should regard being the slave of a religious master the greatest calamity that could befall me. For of all slaveholders with whom I have ever met, religious slaveholders are the worst." Somehow, in *their* hands, God sanctioned cruelty, and Douglass wanted none of it. He had rejected out of hand the resources that Christianity might provide him while he languished in the field pondering certain death. Douglass noted that this crisis called for a prayer of deliverance, but he could not bring himself to pray. Doubts prevented him from "embracing the opportunity, as a religious one."

But in the run-up to the actual conflict with Covey, Douglass experienced a different kind of religious encounter, one that, perhaps, emboldened him to fight. While Douglass hid in a cornfield, a slave named Sandy stumbled upon him and introduced him to something old, mysterious, and powerful:

> I found Sandy an old advisor. He told me, with great solemnity, I must go back to Covey; but that before I went, I must go with him into another part of the woods, where there was a certain *root*, which, if I would take some of it with me, carrying it *always on my right side*, would render it impossible for Mr. Covey, or any other white man, to whip me.

Here, with breathtaking economy, Douglass introduces to the reader a different religious world, one that existed co-extensively with the dominant forms of Christianity. Sandy was a *conjurer*. Conjure is "a magical tradition in which spiritual power is invoked for various purposes, such as healing, protection, and self-defense." Douglass described Sandy as a religious man who combined his faith with "a system for which I have no name." Sandy was also "a genuine African" who "had inherited some of the so-called magical powers said to be possessed by eastern nations."

Magic, no matter Douglass's view of its effectiveness, played a critical part in the world of slaves. Here the distinction between the natural and supernatural collapsed as the world revealed itself as thoroughly enchanted and allied, potentially at least, with good or harm. Sandy entreated Douglass to take hold of the root with a slight riff on Blaise Pascal's wager: that "it could do no harm if it did no good." What followed was a newfound boldness and a willingness, whether inspired by the root or not, to risk his life in battle with Covey. Douglass later rejected the relevance of what he called "divination." But his willingness to unveil the presence of conjure in the world of American slavery points us to a complicated religious landscape in which easy distinctions between magic and religion fall apart.

Conjure expressed a religious worldview that enabled African American slaves to see themselves apart from white slaveholders. It is an African-derived spirituality that empowered its practitioners, through special knowledge, to garner some semblance of control over their environment. This special knowledge did not require rejecting Christianity or other religions of the book—Islam or Judaism. In most cases, practices of conjure stood alongside or within religious expressions readily recognized as Christian. Some charms or spells even used the Bible explicitly.

The use of magic is not unique to African-descended people. Magic, the ability to possess a special knowledge to affect the outcomes of daily living, has been an important feature of the social landscape of all human beings. One can readily see its presence in all facets of American life. For African Americans, conjure presupposes a vast knowledge about the natural and supernatural world, knowledge rooted in an African past disrupted by the transatlantic slave trade and transformed by the institution of slavery in the New World. Here, "Africa" speaks through accumulated wisdom about an enchanted world that held black folk as slaves. That wisdom became a resource for maintaining a sense of humanity under captive conditions.

Magic, religion, and American slavery

The distinction between magic and religion has been a central feature of the study of religion since its inception. Magic became a way to account for the difference between so-called primitive cultures and that of the West. Maritime exploration had opened up the insulated world of what would become Europe, and the encounters of people with different beliefs, ritual practices, and worldviews necessitated a language to differentiate "them" from "us." *They* practiced magic; *we* in the West had religion. In this sense, the very concept of religion played a critical role in fortifying racial meanings about newly encountered people. Religion worked in lockstep with the very idea of differentiating the civilized from the primitive (a distinction critical to the discourse of race in the Western world).

In his classic work *Primitive Culture* (1871), E. B. Tylor noted that the "simple-minded" association of ideas at the heart of magic—that certain primitives believed that they could do harm or heal others by acting on particular objects like clothing or a lock of hair—revealed something fundamental about how human beings made sense of their worlds. Actions that moderns find irrational or outrageous, Tylor suggested, were really efforts on the part of rational actors to shape their worlds in the face of uncertainty. Magic was not wholly different from religion. Rather, its use among primitive cultures was a part of what Tylor referred to as the first "general philosophy of man and nature."

The classicist J. G. Frazer extended Tylor's account of magic in his important work, *The Golden Bough* (1890). For him, magic was much more than a hodgepodge of wild beliefs. It was systematic. Magic connected things that were similar. For example, jaundice, because it produced a yellowish tint of the skin, could be healed by gold because both were of the same color. Magic also connected things on the basis of attachment. Harm could be done by pushing a pin through a doll decorated with the hair of the person to which harm is directed. But for Frazer, even given the systematic nature of magic and the rituals surrounding it, the assumptions of the world informing the practice were wrong: there is no relation between gold and jaundice, and having a lock of someone's hair does not accord one power to harm or heal. This marks the difference between religion and magic. Religion denies the assumptions about causality that animate magical practices. In this sense, for Frazer, religion represents an intellectual advance over magic. Of course, proponents of science would later characterize religion in similar terms.

Emile Durkheim, the French sociologist, distinguished between magic and religion based on their social function not so much on an evolutionary model. For him, magic was primarily utilitarian. Like religion, it involved ideas of the sacred and profane, and rites and beliefs communally shared by others. Those ideas framed how one engaged in certain ritual practices and how others understood their role and function in their social worlds. But, unlike religion, Durkheim argued, magic was primarily a private, individual affair. Magic was all about securing good or doing harm on the basis of personal aims and ends. Religion was different—it is principally social. Religion establishes bonds between otherwise separate individuals and to the society at large by way of an abiding concern with the sacred that gives collective life meaning and significance. Magic does none of this. As Durkheim writes,

"[M]agic has no lasting bonds that make [individual] members of a moral body like the ones formed by worshippers of the same god."

But even with Durkheim's social concerns, in the context of European expansion the distinction between magic and religion works to create a sliding scale between "them" and "us." If different peoples were like us, then the task was to determine in what ways the likeness evidenced itself. But if they were unlike us, "then a host of other designators was at hand for naming the newly found alien peoples along with some of their beliefs, behaviors and institutions —apostasy, paganism, superstition, and magic." The ascription of the use of magic to a people carried with it the weighty designation of "other." And this is a crucial insight. Magic is not simply a private individual affair as Durkheim suggests. The term works within a broader process of distinguishing groups of people and establishing hierarchies among them. Magic also works in the other direction. Those groups who have been designated as "other" or "inferior" can take the practice of magic as their unique possession, which sets them apart from white colonizers or enslavers (where the "us" in question is not white folks but those who have been described as alien).

Magic escapes the "know-how" of the other (in this case, the slaveholder). As one slave said in the 1840s, "I knows t'ings dat de wite folks wid all dar larnin nebber fin's out, an nebber sarches fo' nudder." Or, as Silvia King, an ex-slave interviewed at the age of one hundred, said, "White folks just go through de woods and don't know nothing." In the cornfield, Sandy gave Douglass access to a secret knowledge that initiated him into the insight that Covey was not one of "us." This was not simply an individual act of avoiding harm. It was a social practice that connected Douglass, even if he rejected its value, to Sandy and to a broader sense of the collective life of slaves apart from white slaveholders.

Durkheim's idea that magic is essentially private can make sense within the setting of American slavery only if we leave aside the broader context in which the word characterizes inside and outside, civilized and primitive, "us" and "them." When those who are designated as inferior or primitive actively embrace magic, the distinction between religion and magic collapses. Here the purpose is not to distinguish the civilized from the primitive (who is like us and who is not); instead, the aim is to secure, by means of multiple supernatural sources, possession of a self that cannot be unduly harmed by the circumstances of living. Here magic becomes a practice of freedom.

We can think about this on a macro social level or at the micro level of individual acts. According to his fellow slaves, Gullah Jack, an Angolan-born conjurer who participated in Denmark Vesey's slave insurrection in 1822, fortified the spirits of his co-conspirators with root work. One slave noted:

> [H]e gave me some dry food, consisting of parched corn and ground nuts and said eat that and nothing else on the morning it breaks out, and when you join us as we pass put into your mouth this crab-claw and you can't then be wounded....Jack said he could not be killed, nor could a white man take him.

Whether Gullah Jack was right about the power of the root is not the point. The fact remains that its presence and use affected how those who believed in its power responded to their condition as slaves. They rebelled.

An example on the individual level of the power of magic to secure possession of a self can be seen in the life of Dinkie, a slave conjurer in William Wells Brown's slave narrative, *My Southern Home*. Brown describes Dinkie as a powerful figure who wore a snake's skin, carried a petrified frog in his pocket, and who called forth fear and admiration among his fellow slaves and among white slaveholders. He moved about relatively freely, and even white people sought his counsel about their futures and illnesses. As Brown wrote, Dinkie "was his own master." And, to the extent that he was a slave, Dinkie's assertion of autonomy constituted a powerful, albeit limited, political act.

Conjure can certainly be understood in terms other than its political effects. Spells, roots, and mojo hands happened in the context of actual lives. Folks wanted to harm others, or to convince someone to fall in love with them, or to heal a disease. But if we are to understand conjure as an instance of African American religion, then we must give attention to the political work that the term singles out. Magic conjures up a space for free people or at least folks who have some semblance of control over themselves and their environment. Conjure does this in a world that tries desperately, by marking the slave as primitive and inferior, to deny them that possibility.

We see examples of conjurers in African American slave narratives. They show up in African American folklore as trickster figures or larger-than-life personalities (like Big John or High John the Conqueror) that defy social constraints. In each instance, conjurers act on their worlds, transforming circumstances, escaping danger, and upending standing assumptions about how the world should work. Conjurers revealed a different kind of agency among African American slaves and their descendants. They offered a sense of control in what was otherwise an absurd situation. And, perhaps, their presence exposed a connection to "a way of seeing and being" supposedly lost in the violence of the transatlantic slave trade.

"Africa" and conjure

Sandy "was a genuine African." His advice spoke beyond the dangers of the moment and connected Douglass to an "African" wisdom. It is important to recognize that the spirit of the New World enveloped the presence of all of those Africans forcibly brought from their homelands. Until the 1840s, more Africans crossed the Atlantic than Europeans. By the end of the Atlantic slave trade in 1867, what would amount to 350 years of trafficking black bodies, between 10 and 12 million Africans were transported to the New World. The majority (95 percent) found themselves subject to the brutal labor discipline of sugar plantations in Brazil and the Caribbean. There an early death was their fate, which required the constant replenishing of slave labor.

The fact that Africans were continuously brought to these regions (slavery did not end in Brazil until 1888) aided in the retention of African cultural practices. Approximately 5 million slaves were brought to Brazil and between 2 million and 3 million to the British Caribbean. They brought their gods and their cultural knowledge with them.

Only 6 percent of the total number of captured Africans (some 500,000) made their way to British North America and to what would become the United States. Slavery in the United States, then, took a different path. After 1808 slave labor was primarily produced domestically. This fact sheds light on the gendered dimensions of the slave experience. In the United States, African women worked not only in the fields; their wombs were also sites for the reproduction of slave labor. Here sex and labor became intimately connected, revealing how the reproductive lives of enslaved black women were critical to the institution of slavery in the New World.

Although those 500,000 Africans were brought to North America (the majority of whom arrived between 1720 and 1760), by the time of emancipation in 1865 there were nearly 4 million newly freed slaves, most of whom had little to no immediate knowledge of African cultural practices. Many had experienced, between 1810 and 1861, the brutal consolidation of the plantation regime with its economy of domestic slave trading. Unlike in Brazil and the Caribbean, slave communities in the United States were not regularly infused with the habits and mores of "saltwater" Africans. Expressions of African religiosity were constantly policed; drums, often a means of communication and a source of religious worship among ethnic groups in Africa, were banned; and living memories of "home" faded with each new child born into slavery.

Slavery in the United States did not completely wipe away remnants of a former way of life. Instead, it created the conditions for their transformation. These captured Africans brought to the new world their frames of reference—their gods, their knowledge of rice cultivation, an understanding of the healing and harming powers of nature, their own sense of the mystery and meaning of death, their sense of rhythm and time, their sense of taste and use of spices—and contributed to the development of colonial societies. To be sure, that contribution varied. In places like Brazil, we can clearly see the survivals of African culture in religious practices like *Candomble*, or in Cuba in *Santeria*, or in Haiti in *Voodoo*. In the United States that presence has been less pronounced. Nevertheless, Africa's presence was still felt in the slaves' ring shout, a form of worship in which slaves moved counterclockwise in a circle while shuffling their feet and clapping their hands (see chap. 3). It was seen in ecstatic forms of worship as the enslaved danced and shouted in praise. And it continued to exert influence on the way slaves made sense and interacted with their world through magic.

This view does not presuppose an idea of a black sacred cosmos, which connects the religious imaginings of African-descended people across the globe. In fact, one of the horrible effects of slavery is the erasure in the imagination of the West of the vast ethnic diversity of the African continent itself. In the bowels of slave ships were not Africans with some coherent and jointly held worldview, but were people who identified themselves as Ibo, Teke, Ambundu, Akan, and Fon, with particular histories that shaped how they saw the world and understood themselves. The journey across the Atlantic—one of displacement and dismemberment—transformed them into "Africans" and their homeland into something called "Africa." That transformation left us an "imaginative geography" that helped make sense of the terrible wound/disruption that was slavery. "Africa," in all of its diversity, spoke implicitly and explicitly even in the quarters of those slaves who remembered little or knew nothing of that past. Those fragmented memories and gestures would be passed on from generation to generation. Conjuring then echoes a way of knowing and seeing informed by a cultural repository, both real and imagined, transformed by the institution of slavery in the New World.

African American conjure

Conjuring practices are modes of magical transformation of an inhabited world. They entail healing and harming traditions as well as the use of language and symbols. That is, conjure can help remedy disease and can cause harm to others by way of possession of particular knowledge evidenced in the casting of spells and the appropriate performance of ritual acts. In some ways, conjure offers an account of the world as it is in relation to forces that are not readily seen. It rejects any strict separation between the supernatural and natural world. Instead, we confront an order in which human beings are not passive objects moved about by spirits and the like, but which stand as integral parts of the world as it is. To the extent that human beings are a part of an enchanted world, if they are to secure their happiness and avoid evil, they must acquire an understanding of and an ability to read the signs of that world. In the context of American slavery, conjure offered a measure of control, a means to navigate an environment that was not "accidental or haphazard" and a pathway to assert one's will by imposing some degree of "predictability on a hostile and capricious environment."

Douglass's Sandy is just one example of the conjurer in slavery. William Wells Brown observed that "nearly every large plantation had at least one, who laid claim to be a fortune teller, and who was

regarded with more than common respect by his fellow-slaves."
White missionaries also complained about the pervasiveness of
what they termed "pagan darkness, idolatry and superstition."
In 1842, for example, the Presbyterian minister and missionary
Charles C. Jones noted that slaves "believe[d] in second-sight, in
apparitions, charms, witchcraft, and in a kind of irresistible
Satanic influence. The superstitions from Africa have not been
wholly laid aside." What Jones witnessed was indeed part of the
complex religious world of African American slaves.

Conjure afforded the slave practitioner a way of making sense
of evil and of controlling her immediate environment. It also
provided a way of mitigating the violence of slavery and a means
of engaging fellow slaves that revealed a world apart from the
demands of the master. Conjurers would offer charms that
purportedly prevented masters from whipping their slaves.
We saw this with the root that Sandy gave Douglass. There were
also methods or tools to figure out whether a slave would be the
object of the master's violence. For example, the former slave
Silvia King recounted a story of a slave named Old black Tom
who used what was called a "jack," a small bottle filled with
roots, water, and sulfur, to determine whether someone was to
be flogged. King stated:

> Old black Tom have a li'l bottle and have spell roots and water in it
> and sulphur. He sure could find out if a nigger goin' get whipped.
> He have a string tie round it and say, "By sum Peter, By sum Paul,
> by de God dat made us all, Jack don't tell me no lie, if Marse goin'
> whip Mary, tell me." Sure's you born, if dat jack turn to de left, de
> nigger get de whippin, bit if Marse aint make up he mind to whip,
> dat jack stand and quiver.

Louis Hughes, an ex-slave who lived on plantations in Mississippi
and Tennessee, carried a leather bag with "roots, nuts, pins, and
some other things," which supposedly prevented him from being
whipped. Henry Bibb recounts in his autobiography, *Narrative of*

the Life and Adventures of Henry Bibb, An American Slave,
written by Himself, how a conjurer provided him with protection
from his master's wrath. The conjurer gave him some powder to
sprinkle and a root to chew, and this would prevent him from ever
getting whipped. In some cases the conjuring practice was even
more direct. The ex-slave Mary Middleton tells a story of a slave
who was beaten so badly that she visited a conjurer. The next
morning the master seemed in excellent health, but as the dusk
began to settle his health waned. "As soon as de sun was down, he
down too, he down yet. De witch done dat."

But the object of conjuring practices was not only the master or
the slaveholder. Conjure was also directed at fellow slaves. Here
the individual dimension of the practice comes into view as
people drew on their special knowledge to acquire certain ends,
to heal diseased bodies, or to harm perceived enemies. Charms
dotted the landscape as conjurers sought to achieve their desired
aims. Here we see the full humanity of the slave community in
which jealousies, hatred, and envy animated the lives of slaves.
The record is replete with stories of harming practices that some
say accounted for their inability to walk, the loss of a husband,
the failure of a particular financial venture. For example,
Rosanha Frazier, an ex-slave born in Mississippi, claimed that she
lost her sight because of hoodoo: "Dey powder up de rattle offen
de snake and tie it up in de little old rag bag and dey do devilment
with it. Dey git old scorpion and make bad medicine. Dey git dirt
out de graveyard and dat dirt, after dey speak on it, would make
you go crazy."

Conjure could indeed harm or heal. Silvia King said that the
shoestring root was powerful and strong: "Iffen you chews on it
and spits a ring around de person what you want somethin' from,
you goin' get it. You can get more money or a job or almost
anythin' dat way." Obviously, folks and circumstances could be
manipulated and used for various purposes. Within this economy
of meanings, it was important to know and to see what was

happening around you. One ex-slave summarized the basic logic of conjure in this way: "to catch a spirit, or to protect your spirit against the catching, or to release your caught spirit—this is the complete theory and practice of hoodoo."

Just as conjure could harm it was also a source of powerful healing. Zora Neale Hurston, in her wonderful book *The Sanctified Church*, catalogued a few curative practices that were carried forward into the twentieth century. If one suffered from whooping cough, you were told to "eat fried crow meat, or drink a tea made of sheep manure." If your nose started to bleed, dropping a set of keys down your back would stop the bleeding. Or if you suffered from general afflictions, you were directed to "visit the corpse of one you have known in life, and who was always

2. **A grave covered with various domestic items: clock, cup, goblet, and pots. Fetishes, amulets, and items found in the natural world were thought to be imbued with special healing powers and were used as vessels by many African Americans to implore dead family members for protection and guidance for the living.**

pleasantly disposed toward you. While no one is looking whisper the name of the deceased, and kindly request that he take your affliction along with him." All of which revealed a special knowledge that addressed the body/spirit (because neither was separable).

In the end, conjure played a critical role in the religious imagination of slaves. Whether or not they believed in it, the presence of the conjurer affected how they grabbed hold of the world around them. Conjure offered resources for the daunting task of sense-making, of dealing with the mysteries and disappointments of life with a little more than luck. It provided a little elbow room to imagine freedom and power apart from white slaveholders. But conjure cannot be located solely as a feature of the slave's religious imagination; it is not a relic of a long, forgotten past.

Conjuring practices continued to thrive after slavery and became an integral part, in spite of appeals to respectability and condemnations of heathenism, of the religious landscape of black America. We see it practiced in the southern belt in the late nineteenth and early twentieth centuries; we find it in Spiritualist churches in Chicago and Detroit, a movement that combined elements of Protestantism, Catholicism, and Voodoo. One can even see its presence in the popular imagination. From Richard Pryor's hilarious skit about the witch, Ms. Rudolph, to Charles Burnett's brilliant film *To Sleep with Anger* (1990) or Julie Dash's epic film *Daughters of the Dust* (1991) to Ayana Mathis's novel *The Twelve Tribes of Hattie* (2012), conjuring practices continue to thrive in black America.

Conjure has even touched my own life. In one of our dusty photo albums, there is an old picture of me in bed. I have looked at this photo for well over thirty years—mostly to remember the "old house" on Rose Drive in Moss Point, Mississippi. I am lying down in the bottom bunk with a white rag tied around my head. I was about eight years old, and I had the mumps. Zora Neale Hurston described a cure for the mumps in *The Sanctified Church*: "Vigorously rub the affected area with the marrow obtained from the jowl of a hog. Sardines are also a good cure. The sardines should be eaten by the patient, and the oil rubbed into the affected parts." After reading Hurston recently, I called my mother.

I asked, "Momma, you remember this picture of me in the bed with the mumps with a white rag tied around my head?"

"Yea," she replied.

"I just read about this home remedy. Did you rub sardine oil on my face?"

This devout African American Catholic woman from the coast of Mississippi replied with a slight laugh, "I sure did."

Chapter 3

African American Christianity: The early phase (1760–1863)

Imagine this scene. An Anglican missionary in South Carolina in the early 1700s works to save the souls of black slaves. He faces numerous obstacles. First, slave owners are deeply skeptical of his efforts. Most could not be convinced that "Negroes and Indians are otherwise than Beasts." Moreover, in the past, British law held that it was illegal to hold a fellow Christian in bondage. And, though colonial lawmakers passed legislation that stated clearly there was no connection between baptism and the status of slaves, slave owners remain suspicious about the conversion of black slaves to Christianity. For them, proselytizing among this population presents a threat to the institution of slavery. What would it mean to welcome *their* property to the fellowship of Christ? Black slaves, they maintain, may develop a sense of self-worth, may think of themselves as equal to whites. They may even organize among themselves and rebel.

Efforts to convert slaves continue. And this same missionary eventually finds himself baptizing slaves. But he fears that they are not truly converting to Christ—that some ulterior motive is at work in their willingness to convert. So, he requires that slaves take an oath before administering the sacrament:

> You declare in the presence of God and before this Congregation that you do not ask for the holy baptism out of any design to free

yourself from the Duty and Obedience that you owe to your Master while you live, but merely for the good of Your Soul and to partake of the Graces and Blessings promised to the members of the Church of Jesus Christ.

Here, among low-country planters as it was throughout the slaveholding colonies, Christianity was shadowed by slavery. If slaves were to enter the body of Christ, they had to do so on the condition that they reconcile themselves to their status as someone's property. Irony abounds.

That Anglican missionary was the Reverend Francis Le Jau. And like most missionaries among slaves, he faced enormous challenges to spreading the Gospel among this captive population. Language barriers between missionaries and African-born slaves, and a general disinterest in the spiritual well-being of slaves blocked the way to successful missions. Peter Kalm, a Swedish traveler to British North America from 1748 to 1751, stated clearly the obstacles facing conversion of the slave population:

> It is...to be pitied, that the masters of these negroes in most of the English colonies take little care of their spiritual welfare, and let them live on in their Pagan darkness. There are even some, who would be very ill pleased at, and would by all means hinder their negroes from being instructed in the doctrines of Christianity; to this they are partly led by the conceit of its being shameful, to have a spiritual brother or sister among so despicable a people; partly by thinking that they should not be able to keep their negroes so meanly afterwards; and partly through fear of the negroes growing too proud, on seeing themselves upon a level with their masters in religious matters.

In light of these concerns, British American Protestants showed little interest in engaging in religious instruction among the slave population. For the first 120 years of racial slavery in British North America, Protestant Christianity barely touched the lives of black slaves (although African Americans were a part of the Roman Catholic Church in America from the beginning).

Urged to live up to their Christian duty by the English Church, and with the formation of the Society for the Propagation of the Gospel in Foreign Parts (SPG) in 1701, efforts among Protestants to convert slaves to Christianity increased. But those efforts were distorted by the pressing need to reconcile Christianity with the institution of slavery. As one pamphlet of the SPG stated: "Scripture, far from making an alteration in Civil Rights, expressly directs that every man abide in the condition wherein he is called, with great indifference of mind concerning outward circumstances." Le Jau's oath then was not an aberration but a direct reflection of an effort to make "religion safe for slavery."

For the most part, African American conversion to Christianity took place against the backdrop of the economic imperative of slavery. As such, American Christianity has been indelibly shaped by what the historian David Wills describes as "the encounter between black and white," the domination of slave by free, and that encounter has involved, among other things, a vacillation between an embrace of the abolition of slavery on Christian grounds and a justification for slavery on those same grounds. Here the typical American religious story of Puritans in New England or the narrative about religious pluralism and toleration in the middle colonies take a backseat to the brutal and ironic reality of slavery and Christianity in a place committed, ostensibly at least, to democratic principles.

The encounter between black and white was marked by a radical difference: the gap or distance between Southern whites and African-descended slaves. Not only was this distance cultural—that the slave looked different, talked differently, and acted differently, what Alexis de Tocqueville described in his classic 1835 book, *Democracy in America*, as "this stranger brought into our midst—is hardly recognized as sharing the common features of humanity. His face appears to us hideous, his intelligence limited, and his tastes low; we almost take him for being intermediate between beast and man." The reality of power and the profound prejudice that attended the exercise of that power characterized the gap between black and white.

The system of slavery sought to reduce the slave to mere chattel. It attempted to deprive her of personality and agency, and generated a host of meanings about who the slave was and what were her capacities that affected her relationship and her children's children's relationship with whites. African American Christianity takes its initial shape in this moment: in the distance between professed belief in the Gospel and in the practice of slavery and the ideology of white supremacy.

Not until after 1760 and up to the 1830s was there widespread conversion of slaves to Christianity. Prior to this period, the ambivalence about religious instruction and the accommodation of Christianity with slavery blocked the way to successful missions among slaves. Missionaries often told slave owners that Christian slaves made better slaves. They cited biblical verses such as Ephesians 6:5, where St. Paul says, "Slaves be obedient to them that are your masters according to the flesh, with fear and trembling, in singleness of your heart, as unto Christ" (KJV). Many slave owners came to believe that religion worked as a means of control. But this same religious impulse also served as a basis for what would later become the abolitionist movement as many white Christians viewed slavery as an affront to God. In 1818 Presbyterians announced at their General Assembly, "We consider the voluntary enslaving of one part of the human race by another as a gross violation of the most precious and sacred rights of human nature; as utterly inconsistent with the law of God...and as totally irreconcilable with the spirit and principles of the Gospel of Christ."

Other Christians found no contradiction between their commitment to the Gospel and to the institution of slavery. In 1837, for example, the Reverend Charles C. Jones published a

Catechism directed, in part, to slaves. Among other matters, he listed what was expected of servants in a section titled "Duties of Masters and Servants."

Q. What are the Servants to count their masters worthy of?

A. All honour.

Q. How are they to try to please their Masters?

A. Please them well in all things, not answering again.

Q. Is it right for a Servant when commanded to do anything to be sullen and slow, and answering his master again?

A. No.

Q. But suppose the Master is hard to please, and threatens and punishes more than he ought, what is the Servant to do?

A. Do his best to please him.

Q. Are Servants at liberty to tell lies and deceive their Masters?

A. No.

Q. If servants faithfully do their duty and Serve God in their stations as Servants, will they be respected of men, and blessed and honoured of God, as well as others?

A. Yes.

A Methodist minister asked a slave in Alabama this catechistic question: "What did God make you for?" The answer: "To make a crop."

Frederick Douglass spoke directly to those white Christians who reconciled their religious beliefs with the institution of slavery. In 1846, before a capacity crowd in London, Douglass levied a full frontal assault on the Christian justification for slavery. He thundered, "There has not been any war between the religion and the slavery of the South." He went on to say, "the church and the slave prison stand next to each other...the church-going bell and the auctioneer's bell chime in with each other; the pulpit and the auctioneer's block stand in the same neighborhood." The hypocrisy was glaring.

But African Americans converted to Christianity in relatively large numbers during the Great Awakenings of the eighteenth and early nineteenth centuries. The revivals emphasized individual experience and ecstatic worship. The preachers held that all were equal before God. The revivals became important vehicles for reshaping Christianity in the image of the common folk. Religious leaders had to be unpretentious; the experience of God's grace was available to anyone without mediation; religious instruction was clear and direct; and churches were in the hands of those who attended them. One of the distinctive features of this period was the democratization of the emerging nation's religious life, the result of which was a fascinating fragmentation of the religious landscape as different and independent interpretations of the Gospel resulted in a proliferation of religious groups.

In these revivals, African Americans sat alongside white Christians, and together they experienced the power of God's word and the transforming quality of his presence. White and black alike groaned and cried out as they felt the power of God's presence. This emphasis on immediate experience—that the emotional worship services resembled African forms of religious expression, that many of the revival preachers licensed black preachers, and that early on Baptists and Methodists condemned slavery—resulted in the conversion of large numbers of African Americans.

The Methodist General Conferences of clergy and lay leaders strongly condemned slavery in 1780, 1783, and 1784. They prohibited their ministers from owning slaves and eventually extended that prohibition to the membership in general. The Methodist conference of 1787 urged preachers to work diligently

3. Black slaves and white Christians prayed and sang together at revivals or camp meetings. Common in frontier communities during the Great Awakenings of the eighteenth and early nineteenth centuries, these meetings allowed dispersed Christians to come together in a communal setting.

on behalf of African Americans, "for the spiritual benefit and salvation of the negroes." The General Committee of Virginia Baptists also condemned slavery in 1789 "as a violent deprivation of the rights of nature." But the egalitarian impulses of the revolutionary era soon gave way to the logic of "King Cotton." As these once-marginal religious groups became more mainstream, they divided over the issue of slavery, foreshadowing what would happen in 1861. Ironically, at the very moment African Americans forged a distinctive Christian witness, many evangelical white Christians once again accommodated their Christian beliefs with slavery.

The early phase of African American Christianity is defined by two distinctive tendencies: the significance of the "invisible institution" in the slaveholding South, and the emergence of independent black denominations in the North. In the Southern interior,

African American Christianity took the form of an invisible institution. On the Southern seaboard, black religious expression was more visible but constantly policed by a white, and fearful, gaze. In the North, the maturation of black communities began, with independent black denominations like the African Methodist Episcopal (AME) Church and the African Methodist Episcopal Zion (AMEZ) Church.

The first independent black Baptist congregations, however, were formed not in the North but in the South in the latter part of the eighteenth century. The African Baptist Church on the William Byrd Plantation in Mecklenberg, Virginia, was founded in 1758, and between 1773 and 1775 a slave named George Liele organized the Silver Bluff Baptist Church on the South Carolina bank of the Savannah River. Liele later gained his freedom and preached in Savannah, Georgia, even baptizing several slaves, before leaving for the island of Jamaica around 1783. One slave named Andrew Bryan began to preach in the early 1780s and organized a small group of his fellows to worship outside Savannah in the First African Church in 1788. Two other churches eventually emerged from this congregation.

Most black churches conducted their ministries under the watchful eyes of white slave owners. Andrew Bryan, for example, was whipped on two occasions for holding illegal meetings. He "told his persecutors that he rejoiced not only to be whipped, but would freely suffer death for the cause of Jesus Christ." Many whites believed that independent gatherings fomented slave insurrections and were deeply suspicious of their presence within their communities. As independent gatherings were frowned upon, slaves were permitted to attend the churches of their white masters or churches pastored by white clergy. There the accommodation of Christianity with the peculiar institution would be on full display as white ministers urged the slaves in attendance to "serve your masters.... Do whatsoever your master tell you to do."

Vigilant surveillance characterized the economic system of slavery. Slaves were required to carry passes to move from plantation to plantation. They could not display any sense of individual agency or autonomy that would threaten the foundations of the institution. To do so was to risk severe punishment, such as "the lash" or being sold away from loved ones. The execution of this punishment did not differentiate between male and female slaves, and produced pronounced ideas about black women's bodies as ungendered and as sites for capital accumulation (that is, wombs for the reproduction of slave property). Here the interlocking of labor, sex, race, and violence would undergird the particular experiences of black women's oppression long after slavery was abolished.

Given the surveillance and its potential consequences, many slaves were forced to worship in secret—to steal away to worship God apart from the gaze of white slave owners. And it is here, in the brush arbors and cabins of slaves, that black Christians forged a singular style of worship and a distinctive theological outlook to speak to their unique experiences. That distinctive theology offered those who "took up the cross" an empowering language to see beyond their present condition and to imagine a future defined by freedom, not by slavery or white supremacy. This open-endedness became a signature feature of African American Christian practice, which indelibly shaped African American cultural and political life.

Most black preachers offered a different reading of the Gospel, one that did not accommodate the system of slavery, and preached that slaves, despite their wretched condition, were in fact the chosen people of God. In the story of Exodus, black preachers found an analogy to their captive condition. African Americans emerged in their powerful sermons as the Israelites and America as Egypt, a house of bondage. As slaves gathered and prayed together, like Joshua's army chanting down the walls of Jericho, they danced the "ring shout." Swaying back and forth without allowing their feet to leave the ground, they clapped and sang until everyone "caught the spirit." Here the brutality of slavery was held at arms length, and the spirit was fortified as slaves conversed with Christ and found power in God's love and grace. Slave spirituals conveyed the unshakable resolve that all was not settled as they colored the hymnals of Baptists and Methodists a deep shade of blue.

The haunting sounds from these meetings made audible a profound sadness and an inexplicable joy and confidence. The slave spirituals stood as a musical language that gave voice to the conflicted experience of being a Christian slave:

4. The "ring shout," a common practice in the religious worship of enslaved African Americans, is still practiced by the Gullah, or descendants of slaves living in southern coastal regions. It allowed men and women to stomp and shout in order to facilitate a transcendent spiritual experience. Here, the woman (*left*) demonstrates the correct position of arms and feet in shouting.

> Nobody knows the trouble I've seen
> Nobody knows my sorrow
> Nobody knows the trouble I've seen
> Glory Hallelujah

The troubles of today dimmed in the face of the promise of tomorrow. In short, Christian slaves imagined a new world by drawing on the language of the Gospel and in doing so transcended their captive experience. As one slave noted, "my body may belong to the master but my soul belongs to Jesus." Such imaginings put in place the conditions for Christian slaves to see themselves beyond the relationship of slave and master. They also enabled the slave to reach backward into the world of the early Christians (as well as that of the children of Israel) and blur the lines between the experience recounted in scripture and their own.

Here we see the political significance of African American Christianity. Apart from questions of whether the practice of Christianity among slaves was otherworldly (an escapist fantasy that left the power relation of slavery intact) or this-worldly (a revolutionary ideology that upended the peculiar institution), the religion provided tools to create a sense of personhood—a means to step outside of a relation of domination that sought to reduce human beings to mere chattel—and offered a theology of history in which freedom was possible because of God's very activity in the lives of his chosen people. In prayer meetings and in fellowship with other like-minded Christians, slaves forged a sense of identity, created meaning in the context of an absurd existence, grabbed hold of an idea of freedom rooted in the power of God's love and, in the process, left an indelible mark on the expression of Christianity in the United States.

The Christian witness of those who were enslaved combined with developments among free African Americans in the North. After the American Revolution, slavery gradually disappeared in the North between 1777 and 1818, and African Americans, emboldened by the guarantee of religious freedom, created religious institutions and practiced their faith independent of their white fellows. For many, the reality of racism overshadowed their previous experiences of Christian fellowship. They found themselves all too often segregated into "nigger pews," served communion only after whites were served, denied access to church burial grounds, and refused the rite of christening for their babies. Between 1790 and 1820 then, African Americans founded churches and established denominations where they could worship and have fellowship without the burden of white Christian racism.

Most historical accounts of independent black churches in the North begin with Bethel AME Church in Philadelphia. The church was founded in 1798. Bethel emerged after a racial incident in St. George's Methodist Episcopal Church in Philadelphia. Around 1792, black members of St. George's were told that they could not sit in their usual seats and were ordered to sit in the balcony at the rear of the church. Members complied. But, as the opening prayer began, white ushers insisted that Absalom Jones, despite his requests to finish prayer, get up and move to the back. After prayer was over, Jones rose and along with all of his fellow black members, including Richard Allen, walked out of the church. According to black lore, this moment stands as the founding act of African American Christendom. In 1794, Jones became the pastor of St. Thomas African Episcopal Church in Philadelphia, an independent black church within the larger Episcopal denomination. But Richard Allen, along with many of his fellow black Methodists, left altogether and founded the AME Church in 1816. In 1821 black Methodists in New York City, led by James Varick and Abraham Thompson, would also leave and form what came to be known as the AMEZ Church after continued conflict over the ordination of black preachers.

Like black Methodists, black Baptists also faced white Christian racism. In Boston, for example, black Baptists organized the African Baptist Church in 1804 and appointed the Reverend

Thomas Paul as their pastor. Paul also helped organize the Abyssinian Baptist Church in New York City in 1808. Although these churches maintained active relations with white Baptist churches—and in the case of the Boston congregation, joined the Boston Baptist Association in 1812—they nevertheless came into existence because of the prevalence of white racism within denominational arrangements. The fact that some white Christians believed that the color of their skin deemed them superior in the eyes of God compelled African Americans to seek out a space for the free and autonomous worship of God.

The institutions they created not only provided space for worship but also constituted the beginnings of black civil society. Schools, mutual aid societies, athletic clubs, libraries, insurance companies, and general social events would eventually be housed in black churches. Moreover, these churches became the principal sites for black political life. Within their walls, African Americans addressed the economic realities of their communities and the continued scourge of slavery. Here pastors and worshippers articulated an idea of freedom as they grappled with the pressing implication of slavery in the South. Indeed, the very insistence on the independence of black churches gave content to the idea of freedom insofar as a degraded people took hold of their faith for their own aims and purposes. Black Christians, even among those free African Americans in the North, understood that their witness as Christians was bound up with their status as a "captured people." They did not have a choice but to express their commitment to Christ in terms of a demand for freedom, and this demand for liberation distinguished their understanding of Christianity from that of their white fellows.

Of course, these spaces reflected the internal contradictions of black communities. Interdenominational rivalries emerged as black churches grew, and class and gender differences affected how they conducted political business. Ideas of respectability joined with gendered assumptions about the role of women in public spaces. Ironically, black churches became the primary sites for the construction of troublesome notions of black masculinity that assumed the subordination of black women. They afforded spaces for conventional patriarchal gender roles that were generally unavailable under slavery as both black men and women were subsumed under the patriarchal authority of the slave master.

In black churches matters were different. Black women were denied ordination and not allowed to participate in what was becoming a kind of national black public life. The irony, of course, rests in the fact that "free women were essential to the founding and development of the antebellum black community and church." Their tireless work behind the scenes in organizing events, fund-raising, missionary work, and in ensuring the daily functioning of the institution situated them as critical actors in black Christendom. That work, however, had to navigate patriarchal assumptions sanctioned by sacred authority. Many male preachers cited Paul's declaration that "Let your women keep silence in the churches." (1 Cor. 14:34) Or, they invoked 1 Timothy 2:12, "But I suffer not a woman to teach, nor to usurp authority over the man."

In 1832, Maria Stewart was the first African American woman to speak to a political gathering of men and women. She, along with a host of others, expanded the very idea of freedom and liberation by insisting on the importance of women's voices. Jarena Lee, one of the first women to preach in the AME Church, challenged directly the idea that women should not preach. Jesus, she argued, died for all human beings. Many others cited Galatians 3:28: "There is neither Jew nor Greek, there is neither bond nor free, there is neither male nor female, for ye are all one in Christ Jesus." Lee along with others like Julia Foote (the first woman ordained as a deacon in the AMEZ Church), Zilpha Elaw (an itinerant preacher who preached missions among slaves), and Rebecca Cox Jackson (an eldress in the Shaker denomination and founder of a

Shaker community in Philadelphia) challenged directly the idea that the Gospel was the possession of men. Their witness inspired others as they openly rejected—as they preached the word of God—assumptions about the inferiority of black women.

However complicated and contradictory, black churches were the primary places for these internal debates and arguments about the nature of black life in the United States—debates and arguments that revealed how patriarchy and sexism animated much of African American church life in particular and African American society in general. Black Christian women had to negotiate the fact that sexism ordered their lives fundamentally as they navigated a racist world in which their labor was exploited. Neither could be separated or cordoned off from the other, and their efforts to address the complexity of their experiences during the early phase of African American Christianity laid the foundations for generations to come.

In the end, the specter of slavery and its collateral effects shaped the contours of African American Christianity in its first phase just as it did for American Christianity more generally. The antislavery fervor of early white Baptists and Methodists (which attracted African Americans to their ranks) gave way to the overwhelming power of slavery. Protestant denominations fractured over this question well before the Civil War and would not reunite until, in some cases, the late twentieth century. Their split over slavery foreshadowed the holy war that was to come. Many African American Christians understood the Civil War as a day of reckoning, a sacred event, and with the news of the Emancipation Proclamation in 1863 and the eventual defeat of the South, they now faced an uncertain future as former slaves and second-class citizens.

Chapter 4

African American Christianity: The modern phase (1863–1935)

The modern phase of black Christianity is marked by three distinctive moments. First, the "invisible institution" emerges out of the shadows of slavery, and northern black denominations extend their mission work to the South as well as abroad. Both result in the nationalization of black Christendom. Second, large numbers of African Americans leave the South (what is known as the Great Migration) and relocate to cities in the North and in the West. Their movement occasioned the appearance of what would be called the "institutional church," a church that has social activism and social services at the heart of its theological mission. And, finally, the black freedom struggle of the twentieth century transformed the substance of African American life and the form and content of black Christendom by ending legal segregation.

Nationalizing black Christendom and the age of Jim Crow

Clearly the Civil War changed America. The South was defeated and its economy collapsed, plunging the region into dire poverty. Class antagonisms hidden beneath the reign of the ruling planter class were now fully in the open as yeomen gave voice to their political and economic aspirations. And, of course, former slaves worked tirelessly to imagine what a life of freedom might look like in a region and a country devastated by war and still committed to white supremacy. Moreover, the execution of the war led to policies that transformed the national life of the country. The unprecedented expansion of federal power resulted in the birth of the modern American state (from the federal government creating a national paper currency and banking system to new taxes on production and consumption to the passage of the Homestead Act and the Land-Grant College Act to government assistance through land grants and bonds that made possible the transcontinental railroad).

Amid these enormous changes stood African Americans longing for a new place in American society. Before the outbreak of the war, African Americans had built institutions in the North and created a way of life, even under the watchful eyes of Southern slaveholders, in the South. African American Christianity played a critical role in both regions, as churches were fertile ground for the cultivation of "freedom dreams." With the Emancipation Proclamation, the end of the war, and the passage of the Thirteenth, Fourteenth, and Fifteenth Amendments to the U.S. Constitution, African Americans were now "free" to build and expand those institutions. Their attention turned to expanding educational possibilities, to securing and stabilizing families, to seeking some degree of economic independence, and to defining clearly a political culture that would serve as the platform to make claims on behalf of the black community. In effect, they put in place the foundations for modern black America.

After the Civil War, Christian missionaries, black and white, descended on the South. What they found were newly freed men and women materially desperate but anxious to step into a new and more modern way of living. They longed for education and for economic independence. Along with the Freedmen's Bureau, missionary organizations like the American Missionary Association provided basic aid and teachers. They built schools, many of which became major black educational institutions. Some of America's most important historically black colleges and universities were founded during this period. Shaw University in Raleigh, North Carolina, was founded in 1865; Morehouse College in Atlanta, Georgia, in 1867; Fisk University in Nashville, Tennessee, in 1866; and Hampton Institute in Hampton, Virginia, in 1868.

Black Christian missionaries, especially African American women, were particularly active in the war-torn South. Indeed the work of black women missionaries laid the foundation for a broader expression of black feminism in the latter part of the nineteenth century and the early twentieth century. Within these organizations, black women held leadership roles, engaged in fund-raising, honed their organizational skills, and challenged explicitly and implicitly gendered assumptions about the role of women in public life generally. As a result of their work and the missions, thousands of former slaves withdrew from predominantly white churches.

Many former slaves left white churches as a declaration of independence and self-determination. But it is important to note the concerted effort by African American Christians to proselytize among this population. The mass exodus of black Christians from white churches amounted to something like a "black religious awakening." Black Christian missions in the South not only convinced many black Christians to leave white churches but also converted large numbers of former slaves to the faith. As a result, black denominations became national institutions during this period as their influence reached across the United States. The AME Church had only 20,000 members in 1856; by 1865 its numbers had grown to 75,000 members, and by 1880 the church claimed membership close to 400,000 members. Other former slaves joined the AMEZ Church. Still others organized in 1870 a new black denomination, the Colored Methodist Episcopal Church (they would later change the name to Christian Methodist Episcopal Church in the 1950s).

Black Baptists, the largest grouping of black Christians, were no different. Like their Methodist counterparts, the end of the war occasioned a mass exodus from white Baptist congregations. They eventually organized the National Baptist Convention (1895) to facilitate more coordinated action among black Baptists in evangelizing and in addressing the pressing needs of black communities. The organization split into two entities in 1915: the National Baptist Convention of the United States of America, Inc., and the National Baptist Convention of America (unincorporated).

This period of enormous growth in black Christendom reflected an unshakable desire to build communities. African Americans, both former slaves and those who knew only freedom, took huge steps to forge a way of life that enabled them to secure a modicum of safety and the possibility of making real their dreams, or at least their children's dreams. Schools, newspapers, civic organizations, and political activism all became features of a black world facing extraordinary change. African American Christianity was critical in their efforts. By the end of the last decade of the nineteenth century, close to 3 million African Americans belonged to some church. This institution, once hidden from view in the South and the cornerstone of black communities in the North, now stood, only forty years or so removed from emancipation, as the most important institutional expression of black life in the country, shaping the black community's moral and political direction for generations to come.

White America did not stand idly by. The presence of freed African Americans in the South stoked resentment and anger. As African Americans sought to consolidate their gains during Reconstruction, as black men voted (reminding black women of the double bind of gender and race) and assumed roles in local, state, and federal government, and as black communities built and fortified their institutions, white supremacy once again reared its ugly head. A reign of white terror brought Reconstruction and its fragile attempt at multiracial democracy to a screeching halt. The Compromise of 1877 removed U.S. troops from the South, exposing African Americans to the extralegal violence of white Southerners. Northern commercial interests sought to exploit the economic potential of this underdeveloped part of the country and its vast resources of cheap labor. Political alliances realigned as agrarian populism, with its potential for multiracial coalitions, collapsed in the face of cyclical economic depressions and as virulent racism eased, at least for the moment, class tensions between whites. In short, African Americans, less than two decades after the end of the Civil War, confronted a national retreat on racial matters.

Many advocates in the North experienced a kind of moral fatigue with regards to racial matters; they capitulated to the racism in the South in part because they too held certain beliefs about the role and place of African Americans in American society. The great southern historian C. Vann Woodward put the point powerfully in his classic book, *The Strange Career of Jim Crow*: "Just as the Negro gained his emancipation and new rights through a falling out between white men, he now stood to lose his rights through the reconciliation of white men." Here the complicity of the entire nation with white supremacy is readily seen. All too often the burden of slavery and legal segregation rests solely on the shoulders of the South—a kind of "southern exceptionalism" in which the region stands apart from the rest of the nation because of its commitments to white supremacy. But the nation as whole allied to disrupt the transition of the status of millions of former slaves to that of free citizens. The real consequences of generations of slavery were all too easily tossed aside as the nation chose to believe that the race question had been resolved or, minimally, was no longer worth the fight between white Americans.

The Supreme Court withdrew legal support for the civil rights of blacks in the South. In the *Slaughter House Cases* of 1873, the court began the process of reinterpreting the Fourteenth Amendment and the idea of black citizenship. In *U.S. v. Reese* and *U.S. v. Cruikshank* in 1875, the Court effectively left the question of the status of black people in the South to be answered by southern white supremacists. The Court ruled that the Civil Rights Act of 1875 was unconstitutional and, in 1896, *Plessy v. Ferguson* established separate but equal as the law of the land. White supremacists were given full license to reassert control over the region and to ensure, both politically and symbolically, that African Americans were second-class citizens. This was the birth of the Age of Jim Crow.

That birth was attended by violent convulsions. As white supremacists reasserted control over the South, many took to extralegal violence as the primary means to "keep the Negro in his place." The dreaded American ritual of lynching emerged as the most brutal expression of that violence. Between 1887 and 1906, an African American in the South was lynched every four days. Some two thousand African Americans in the South were victims of this barbaric practice during this period. On August 21, 1899, in McIntosh County, Georgia, Henry Delegale was about to be a victim of a white mob. Delegale, a prominent African American in the local community, had been accused of rape and was jailed. As the sheriff tried to release him to the mob, the bell of the local black Baptist church began to ring, alerting the black community. Hundreds of African Americans, many of them armed, rushed to the aid of Delegale, who was saved, later tried and acquitted.

All too often white ministers justified the rage of the mobs. In 1903, the Reverend Robert Elwood, pastor of Olivet Presbyterian Church in Wilmington, Delaware, invoked Corinthians 5:13, "Therefore put way from among ourselves that wicked person," as he urged the crowd to take justice in its own hands and lynch George White, who was accused of rape. Elwood was not alone. During this period, many whites intimately connected evangelical Protestantism with white supremacy. So much so that by 1915 a former Methodist minister, George Simmons, revived the Ku Klux Klan in Stone Mountain, Georgia. Members were required to join a Protestant church as the organization explicitly yoked together their defense of the white race with their commitment to Jesus Christ.

As in the case of Henry Delegale, African Americans and their churches were not passive in the face of such hostility. They actively resisted and took up the challenge of providing safety and possibility for themselves and their children. Black preachers responded theologically. They talked about the destiny of African Americans wrapped up in the redemption of Africa and in their unique mission to the world. Some even argued for emigration to Africa. Bishop Henry McNeal Turner of the AME Church wrote in January 1883:

> Matters cannot go on as at present, and the remedy is thought by tens of thousands to be in a negro nationality. This much the history of our world establishes, that races either fossilized, oppressed or degraded must emigrate before any material change takes place in their civil, intellectual, or moral status, otherwise extinction is the sequence.

The suffering that African Americans faced was also accounted for in readings of the book of Job and in invocations of Exodus and of Psalms 68:31. "Ethiopia shall stretch forth her hands to God" was not a fatalistic embrace of the inevitability of God's will. It was a clarion call to actively take up the task of redeeming the world through a particular witness of Christianity—one drenched in the blood of black martyrs who suffered and died at the hands of those who *claimed* to be Christian.

As the roots of Jim Crow took hold in the South, African American Christianity took on a particular shape and tone. The desperation of the times called for a theology that could account for the evil and suffering so pervasive throughout the nation and particularly in the South. That violence—and the failure of the country as a whole to live up to the promises of American democracy—forced African Americans to turn inward. The nation-state refused to protect them. The burdens and benefits of citizenship were denied them. And, yet, they were still charged with creating a distinctive life in the United States.

What is clear is that African Americans did not cower. The end of the nineteenth century and the dawn of the twentieth century saw an increase in black political organizations: the short-lived Afro-American League (1890); the National Council of Negro Women (1896); the American Negro Academy (1897); the National Association for the Advancement of Colored People (1910); and the National Urban League (1911). Each of these organizations sought to expand the very idea of democracy in the United States by dislodging an insidious idea of race, which distorted democratic principles. And all were deeply connected and indebted to African American Christianity.

Black Baptist women organized conventions in the 1880s, with more than a million women attending the first Women's Convention in Richmond, Virginia, in 1900. The convention reflected a broad-based effort among black Baptist women to assert a more prominent leadership role in their churches. African American women represented somewhere between 65 to 90 percent of the membership of black churches. Yet, denied ordination and constrained by the assumptions of domesticity (that the best place for women was in the home), they faced tremendous sexism among black male clergy. These same women, many of whom worked as domestic laborers, were the backbone of fund-raising for domestic and foreign missions.

That work informed more secular efforts to respond to racism and sexism more broadly. Under the leadership of S. Willie Layton and Nannie Burroughs, the black Baptist women of the convention took up the most pressing social and political issues of their times.

They urged a politics of respectability as they challenged African Americans to live morally upright lives. They also challenged segregation in all of its ugly dimensions, especially the terror of lynching. Their work, along with black women in other denominations, challenged prevailing sentiments about black women's roles in public life. Their activism set a tone and laid down a pathway that would influence other organizations in their challenge to Jim Crow and patriarchy in the United States.

Another form of black religious expression emerged during this time as well. In 1885, Charles H. Mason and Charles Jones, two black Baptist ministers, accepted the Holiness doctrine of sanctification and began to preach. That doctrine held that the converted needed to experience a "second work of grace" in which the infilling of the Holy Spirit and the power of God's love liberated one from sin. This emphasis on sanctification produced huge riffs among black Baptists, and Jones and Mason found the doors of many Baptist churches closed to them. Jones would later organize a fellowship known as the Church of God. Two years later in 1887, Jones and Mason organized the Church of God in Christ.

Others, like Charles Parham, a white faith healer and founder of the Apostolic Faith, insisted on the centrality of speaking in tongues as evidence of the presence of the Holy Spirit. This baptism in the spirit or "third work of grace" approximated the Pentecost experience of the New Testament when the disciples of Jesus spoke in "unknown tongues." The new movement became known as Pentecostalism and espoused the belief that the gifts of the spirit evidenced themselves not only in the ability to speak in tongues but in the ability to prophesy, heal, discern, and to interpret.

In 1906 William J. Seymour, a Holiness black preacher who was introduced to the idea of baptism in the Holy Spirit by the pioneering Holiness woman preacher Lucy Farrow (also a student of Parham's), organized a prayer meeting in Los Angeles at 216 Bonnie Brae Street. In a small cramped space folks worshipped and spoke in tongues. The meeting grew in size (after only a week more than two hundred people were in attendance) and changed venues to 312 Azusa Street. For three years the Azusa Street revivals attracted people of all races to experience the power of the Holy Spirit. Charles Mason was among those who were baptized in the spirit. He embraced Pentecostalism and its doctrine of speaking in tongues. Mason described his experience:

> The sound of a mighty wind was in me and my soul cried, "Jesus, only, one like you." My soul cried and soon I began to die. It seemed that I heard the groaning of Christ on the cross dying for me. All of the work was in me until I died out of the old man. The sound stopped for little while. My soul cried, "Oh, God, finish your work with me." Then the sound broke out in me again.... When I opened my mouth to say glory, a flame touched my tongue which ran down me. My language changed and no word could I speak in my own tongue.

Mason returned home to Memphis to preach the doctrine of the third gift of grace. Many rejected his newfound belief, including Charles Jones. Others followed Mason, and his nascent church became what is now the largest black Pentecostal denomination, the Church of God in Christ or COGIC (Jones would rename his faction the Church of Christ, Holiness).

Ironically, black Pentecostalism takes its initial shape in the context of interracial fellowship during a time of immense racial violence. It is the only black denomination that was not founded with an exodus from a white religious organization. In fact, it was the other way around. The interracial fellowship was short lived as white Pentecostals eventually left to form their own religious organizations.

During this period, Pentecostalism introduced a new sound and posture in black religious life. Sanctified individuals saw

5. Pentecostal worshippers lift their hands in praise at a church in Chicago. Pentecostalism espoused the belief that the gifts of the Spirit could be seen in the ability to speak in unknown tongues, prophesy, heal, discern, and interpret.

themselves over and against the world. They refused to dance, drink alcohol, or go to the movies—to engage in any activity that demonstrated an allegiance to "the world." This is not to suggest that Pentecostals were completely silent with regard to the politics of their day, because they were not. It merely notes a disposition that has led many to see them as "otherworldly."

Founding organizations, religious or otherwise, was not the only mode of resistance or assertion of black independence in the face of racial violence. African Americans (women, men, and children) also used their feet as they sought out a Promised Land, a place to exercise their freedom apart from the violence of the South. Early on, Exodusters hopped boats up the Mississippi River to St. Louis, then made their way to Kansas City and Topeka via the Missouri River. That movement foreshadowed what was to come. The trickle of migration of the 1870s became a flood, and that movement fundamentally changed the face of black Christendom. This historic movement of people stood as a profound expression of the power of African American religion as millions of black people struck out on faith for a better life for themselves and for succeeding generations.

The Great Migration

Racial violence in the South, the reality that Jim Crow was fast becoming the law of the land, and catastrophic economic events in the region contributed to the massive departure of more than 2.5 million African Americans from the South between 1890 and 1930. That movement greatly transformed cities throughout the country. Chicago saw its black population increased by 114 percent; more than 65,000 black migrants moved to the city. Detroit experienced a 611 percent increase; Cleveland, 308 percent; New York City 66 percent; Indianapolis, 59 percent; Cincinnati, 54 percent; Pittsburgh, 47 percent. Southern cities like Birmingham also saw significant jumps in their black populations. Between 1900 and 1920 Birmingham experienced a 215 percent increase.

This massive internal movement of the black population coincided with global shifts with the historically unparalleled migrations of people to and within nations (movements associated with fundamental transformations in the nature of capitalism). African Americans from the South entered cities in the North and Midwest and joined migrants from Europe and the Caribbean who made their way to American cities. In 1890, for example, 90 percent of the African American population resided mostly in the rural South. By 1930, 44 percent lived in cities. Between 1860 and 1890, about 10 million immigrants from Europe made their way to American shores (and mostly settled in cities). Between 1890 and 1914 that number soared to 15 million. Black southerners joined this cosmopolitan stew. They brought with them distinctive sounds and styles of worship that added to the diversity of the religious landscape of American cities.

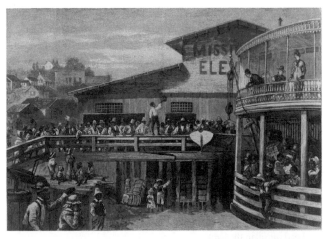

6. In order to escape racial violence and the decline of the plantation economy in the South, "Exodusters" traveled on boats up the Mississippi River toward midwestern cities. The Great Migration contributed to the proliferation of independent black churches in the North and the Midwest.

The Great Migration precipitated the birth of modern gospel music. Most tend to think of the period as one defined by the blues or the literature of the Harlem Renaissance. But black working-class culture, deeply rooted in African American Christianity and shaped by the voices of newly urbanized southerners, ushered in what the historian Evelyn Brooks Higginbotham calls the "Age of Voice." Southerners brought with them a so-called folk orality that fundamentally shaped the soundscape of cities. One heard that sound in Holiness and Pentecostal churches as Sunday services "rocked" with the spirit. One could hear it in the songs of Mother McCollum's "Jesus is My Aer-O-plane" and Sister Calley's "Everybody Get Your Business Right," two little-known women from the rural South who recorded songs once they arrived in Chicago. It was also evident in the genius of Thomas Dorsey, the man widely known as the father of gospel music.

Dorsey, formerly known as "Georgia Tom," was a blues musician who converted to Christ. His conversion resulted in an amazing fusion of sound as the structure of the blues shaped and informed his gospel compositions. Dorsey wrote and sold his sheet music to local choirs, and after becoming the music director of Pilgrim Baptist Church in Chicago, he eventually organized a convention of gospel singers that would formally organize this tradition and ensure its continued success. His powerful composition "Precious Lord" is performed around the world to this day.

> Precious Lord, take my hand
> Lead me on, let me stand
> I'm tired, I'm weak, I'm worn
> Through the storm, through the night
> Lead me on to the light
> Take my hand precious Lord, lead me home.

Dorsey's success was made possible by extraordinary advances in communication and technology, most notably the radio and phonograph. Recording industries emerged around the particular niche market of black consumers. "Race records" included blues and jazz recordings as well as religious sermons. Between 1925 and 1945 Baptist and Pentecostal preachers recorded some seven hundred sermons. Radio stations broadcast religious services and the sermons of black preachers. This technology influenced the experience of church, gave African American Christianity a new kind of mobility, and enabled its advance beyond the bricks and mortar of church buildings. People listened to sermons in the privacy of their homes. They consumed religious doctrine just like they consumed the blues or black hair products. In other words, African American Christianity, reshaped by the presence of southern migrants, entered the circuitry of mass consumer capitalism. Both indelibly shaped the modern phase of African American Christianity.

Traditional mainline black churches also experienced unprecedented growth in their membership due to the migration of black southerners. Albert Tindley's East Calvary Methodist Episcopal Church in Philadelphia saw its active membership increase to more than seven thousand by 1923, and the membership of Ebenezer Baptist Church in Pittsburgh grew from fifteen hundred to close to three thousand between 1915 and 1926. In fact, between 1926 and 1936, black membership in black churches increased to 5.7 million. Black Baptists showed the most remarkable growth. By 1936, they counted 3.8 million black people among their ranks.

This growth resulted in the emergence of what has been called the "institutional church." These were churches of substantial size whose function extended well into the social and economic lives of their members and the community at large. Reverdy C. Ransom, an AME minister, described the institutional church in a 1901 article in the *Christian Recorder*:

> The institutional AME Church in Chicago was not before its time. It comes to meet and serve the social conditions and industrial needs of the people, and to give answers and solutions to many grave problems which confront our Christianity in the great centers of population of our people....It is a teaching, ministering nursing-mother, and seeks through its activities and ministrations to level the inequalities and bridge the chasms between the rich and poor, the educated and the ignorant...and to bring all ages and classes of the community to contribute to the common good.

Churches provided for families in economic need, helped locate housing, delivered day-care services, offered adult education classes and job training. Ministers could not simply focus on the souls of their congregations; their practical needs required attention as well.

The challenges of the Great Migration were enormous and exerted tremendous pressure on the resources and capacities of black religious institutions. Well-established black churches found themselves in rapidly changing economic and social environments. Industrialization and modernization, just as they affected the expression of American Christianity generally, now pressed in on black communities and changed the nature of their experience with markets, with work, and with God. Many churches found themselves the object of severe criticism as some claimed that the institution had fallen out of step with the dramatic structural changes facing black America. It seemed that black churches and preachers were more interested in money and moving into new sanctuaries than they were in the social misery and political exclusion of black communities.

This criticism stood alongside the disenchantment many migrants felt once they arrived in cities. Most southern migrants imagined their journey from the South as a religious one, a journey from Egypt to a promised land of opportunity. But upon arrival, many confronted social and economic misery as they were herded into black ghettos and found themselves in fierce competition with European immigrants who were learning, rather quickly, the privileges of "whiteness" in the United States.

Demographic shifts, dramatic changes in the labor patterns of African Americans, and deepening class stratification within black communities greatly affected the lives of the recent migrants. Combined with the seismic global shifts in the aftermath of the two world wars and the increasing influence of the United States on the world stage, black migrants were moving at a time of domestic and global destabilization and reorganization. They, like so many people, were trying to find their feet in a vastly changing world. And finally, the convulsions within American Christendom did not escape black Christian communities. As battles were waged around doctrine and persons aligned with fundamentalism, with its beliefs about the inerrancy of the Bible, or with liberal Christianity, African American Christians, in their own distinctive ways, expressed doctrinal differences in the very way they oriented themselves, if at all, to political matters.

Those differences were a part of a complex religious marketplace—one that existed in southern cities as well as in northern ones—in which African Americans found themselves with a variety of religious choices. If they did not like the big, impersonal churches, they worshipped in storefronts or in their homes. Some amplified their Christian beliefs by embracing New Thought, a religious science that held the belief that the power of human consciousness directly affects the nature of reality. Others joined groups led by such charismatic figures as Father Divine, the leader of the Peace Mission Movement, and Daddy Grace, the founder of the Universal House of Prayer of All People.

Other organizations offered an alternative Christian piety. Marcus Garvey's movement, the Universal Negro Improvement Association (UNIA), provided disaffected black Christians with a liturgy that affirmed their self-worth and a politics that positioned African Americans as an independent nation. Images of a black Christ and Madonna, even a distinctive catechism (the *Universal Negro Catechism*) aligned Christianity with a kind of piety of blackness. Many simply left Christianity altogether.

Some became black Jews. William S. Crowdy organized the Church of God and Saints of Christ in 1896 and preached that black people were descended from the ten lost tribes of Israel. In 1920, Wentworth A. Matthew formed the Commandment Keepers Congregation of the Living God. Matthew and his followers believed that African Americans were really Ethiopian Hebrews. Others embraced their own version of Islam. In 1913 Timothy Drew, later known as Noble Drew Ali, established the Moorish Science Temple in Newark, New Jersey. Ali taught that African Americans were really "Asiatics," whose homeland was Morocco and their holy book was *The Holy Koran*, a sixty-page book that bears no resemblance to the Qur'an, the holy book of Islam, and shares some of the esoteric teachings of New Thought.

Another organization claimed Islam as the primary religious identity of African Americans. The Nation of Islam was founded in Detroit in 1930 by a mysterious peddler named W. D. Fard. Fard taught that black people were Muslims, descendants of the "lost-found tribe of Shabbazz," and that white people were "devils." He eventually disappeared under questionable circumstances in 1934, and his successor, Elijah Poole, later known as Elijah Muhammad, led the organization until his death in 1975.

In each instance, the religious identities of these organizations were inextricably tied to the political circumstance of black America. Joining these organizations was as much about rejecting America and white Christianity as it was about an expression of a newfound religious faith. The religious marketplace of the early twentieth century, then, reflected the deep racial realities of the nation. It also revealed the enormous religious creativity of African Americans. They were religious bricoleurs of the first order, drawing on a variety of traditions to imagine new ways to be religious in a world organized by white supremacy.

This political dimension is important to any understanding of the modern phase of African American Christianity, and it is clearly expressed in the explosion of civic and religious energy in the middle of the twentieth century that fundamentally transformed the United States: the civil rights movement.

Chapter 5
African American Christianity: The modern phase (1935-1980)

The convulsions of the early twentieth century set the stage for a series of transformations in African American Christianity, the most important of which would be the role black churches would play in the long, modern, civil rights journey. The two world wars thrust the United States onto the international stage, and its economic strength and inventiveness secured the country's place as a global power. The intervening years were quite lean, though. The Great Depression created enormous hardships for the nation, especially for African Americans, who were already among the poorest and most vulnerable Americans. In Harlem, the median income for black families fell by 50 percent. In the South, up to three-quarters of black families turned to public assistance. Father Divine, the charismatic religious leader of the Peace Mission Movement who many believed to have the power to alleviate poverty, held elaborate "banquets" in his communities, which were called "heavens." His ability to offer food in such difficult times stood as proof for many of his unique spiritual status.

But even Father Divine's benevolence extended only so far. Times were rough, and the economic circumstances exacerbated racial tensions. White men in Atlanta marched downtown with signs that read, "Niggers go back to the cotton fields, city jobs are for white folks." As African Americans engaged in the most dramatic population shift in U.S. history, they faced an economic tsunami that wiped away the previous world order.

The Great Depression revealed the fatal flaws of a certain understanding of "free markets," and the federal government stepped in to stabilize matters. Franklin D. Roosevelt's New Deal reimagined the government's role and put forward social democratic policies and limited civil rights reform that resulted in the beginning of a major political realignment. Many African Americans left the Republican Party and joined the Democratic Party (a shift that would be solidified with the passage of the Civil Rights Act of 1964 and the Voting Rights Act of 1965). They did so as their political clout grew in northern cities as black migration increased the size of the black electorate and as black activism intensified throughout the nation.

In 1934, for example, Arthur W. Mitchell of Chicago became the first black Democrat elected to Congress in U.S. history. The NAACP also saw its membership more than triple between 1934 and 1944. And in 1941, A. Philip Randolph, founder of the Brotherhood of Sleeping Car Porters, the first black labor union, along with A. J. Muste and a young Quaker named Bayard Rustin (both members of the pacifist Fellowship of Reconciliation), threatened to mobilize a massive act of civil disobedience in Washington, D.C. What came to be known as the March on Washington movement demanded anti-lynching legislation and the desegregation of the armed forces. In response to the threat, President Roosevelt issued Executive Order 8802 (the Fair Employment Act) banning discrimination in the national defense industry. A new militancy was taking shape in black America.

African Americans from every sector of life were drafted to fight the battle against fascism in World War II. More than 3 million African American men enlisted in the armed services, and close to a half million were deployed in segregated units in Africa, the Pacific, and Europe. The war effort also drafted black men and women at home into factory lines as the stream of European migration was temporarily interrupted. White workers rebelled and "hate strikes" consumed the nation. But the call to fight for freedom and democracy abroad opened up pathways for calls for freedom and democracy at home. Even with the Great Migration, in the decade following World War II, the majority of African Americans, more than 60 percent in fact, still lived in the South. Most African Americans still languished in a region marked by Jim Crow and escalating racial violence. Black organizations and newspapers around the nation pressed the contradiction between the country's rhetoric against Germany and its persistent commitment to racial apartheid at home. Black America was poised to challenge the nation in ways that the country had never before witnessed.

African American churches and Christians were not on the sidelines during this period. To be sure, the Great Migration presented a number of challenges to black churches, and many of these institutions faced stinging criticisms about their purported "otherworldly" approach to the Gospel, self-interested preachers, and insular concerns about church growth. Horace Cayton and St. Clair Drake captured this sentiment in their comprehensive study of Chicago's South Side, *Black Metropolis: A Study of Negro Life in a Northern City* (1945):

> Commanding the allegiance of so many people and handling such a large amount of Bronzeville's money, the church inevitably becomes a matter of public discussion.... The most striking thing about these comments was the prevalence of grumbling against preachers and the church—a habit found among members and non-members alike. The major criticisms ran somewhat as follows: (1) Church is a "racket," (2) Too many churches, (3) There's no real religion among the members, (5) Churches are a waste of time and money, (6) Ministers don't practice what they preach, (7) Ministers don't preach against "sin," (8) churches place too much emphasis on money, (9) Negroes are too religious.

However fair these criticisms may or may not have been, they did not capture the entire range of black Christian activity. Black congregations were involved in every major civil rights organization in the country. The NAACP relied on members of black churches as they organized chapters throughout the South. Black churches provided meeting spaces and resources for mobilization efforts, which challenged legal segregation. Ministers like Howard Thurman worked actively in pursuit of a living Gospel relevant to the particular circumstances of African Americans.

Thurman, born in 1900 in Daytona, Florida, stood as an early proponent of interracial religious cooperation. In 1935 he and his wife, Sue Bailey Thurman, traveled to India with a delegation of African Americans sponsored by the YMCA. There they met Mahatma Gandhi and learned of his philosophy of nonviolence. Thurman also faced a difficult question by one of his Indian hosts. Given the oppression of African Americans by Christians, he was asked, how could he still believe in Christianity? Thurman distinguished Christianity from the "religion of Jesus." Apart from ecclesiastical structures and church dogma, the religion of Jesus espoused "freedom... and justice for all people, black, white, red, yellow, saint, sinner, rich or poor." It rejected the idolatry of whiteness. This distinction served as the principal framework for his influential book, *Jesus and the Disinherited* (1949), and shaped the views of Dr. Martin Luther King Jr.

Rev. J. A. Delaine, a pastor in Summerton, South Carolina, played a crucial role in the historic NAACP case of *Brown v. Board of Education*. Delaine was the principal of the all-black school in Summerton. He petitioned the school board of Clarendon County to provide buses for black students just as they did for white students. The board resisted. The NAACP agreed to step in, and it filed suit for broader equal educational opportunity in Clarendon Country. The case came to be known as *Briggs et al. v. Elliot et al.* Rev. T. J. Jemison and a host of other local black churches, organized under the rubric of the Urban Defense League, led a massive boycott of segregated buses in Baton Rouge, Louisiana, in 1953.

Perhaps more important than the actions of particular male preachers were the active networks of black Christian women and their white allies engaged in social and political activity, which shaped what would become the modern civil rights movement. Churchwomen's organizations such as the National Association of Colored Women, the Young Women's Christian Association, the Women's Missionary Union, and the National Council of Negro Women sought to address the conditions of local black communities. In doing so they laid the foundation for the various forms of interracial cooperation that would shape the civil rights movement of the 1950s and '60s.

Black churches—with black women comprising 65 to 90 percent of the membership—offered networks of interconnection that enabled massive mobilization of people and resources to challenge racial segregation throughout the South. Highlighting this dimension of black churches illustrates that the black freedom struggle of the 1960s was not some spontaneous explosion of civic energy. In so many ways, long-standing efforts to resist racial oppression in the South and throughout the United States revealed *the* distinctive feature of African American Christianity: that this religious tradition acquired its uniqueness insofar as it sought to respond to the racial regime within which it was practiced.

In the totality of the experience of worship, the distinctive cultural origins of African American Christianity were felt. Congregations engaged in call-and-response, shouting "Amen" or "Yes, Lord" as preachers chanted sermons or as fellow churchgoers offered prayers to the Lord. In some churches, this communal experience involved the raising or lining of hymns, where someone would sing a line of a song and the congregation would take it up with

7. The National Association for the Advancement of Colored People (NAACP) relied on members of black churches as they organized chapters throughout the South. Black churches provided meeting spaces and resources for mobilization efforts, which challenged legal segregation.

short, long, and common meter—all with melodic variation. The result was a powerful sonic religious expression. Classic hymns such as Charles Wesley's "A Charge to Keep I Have" were radically transformed by haunting and beautiful arrangements that often left words aside for moans that captured the uneasy relation between the pain and hurt of black life in the United States and the power of God's grace.

The form and content of the early stages of the civil rights movement were deeply indebted to black church practices. The meetings themselves mirrored a liturgy of sorts. Singing and speeches fortified spirits as participants prepared themselves to face the brutal responses of white southerners. The "movement hymns" worked like the spirituals of old:

I ain't gon' let nobody turn me 'round,
Turn me 'round,
Turn me 'round, turn me 'round
I ain't gon' let nobody turn me 'round,
I am gonna keep on a walkin', keep on a talkin',
Walkin' up freedom's land.

Preachers and laypersons offered an inspiring word to frame the anticipated action, and then everyday, ordinary folk (men, women, and in some cases children) risked everything for the prospect of freedom as faith took the form of boycotts, marches, and sit-ins.

In Montgomery, Alabama, in 1955, a young Baptist preacher emerged as a shining example of the political significance of African American Christianity. Martin Luther King Jr. was born in 1929 in Atlanta. He was the first son of one of the leading Baptist ministers in the city, and his grandfather, A. D. Williams, was the second pastor of Ebenezer Baptist Church in Atlanta. King graduated from Morehouse College in 1948. There he encountered the likes of Dr. Benjamin Elijah Mays, the famed president of Morehouse, a University of Chicago–trained theologian and the co-author of *The Negro's Church*. King was also exposed to the spiritual teachings of Howard Thurman. Those influences shaped his theological vision early on. King powerfully articulated the relationship between a living Gospel and the matter of justice. Throughout his public ministry he drew on the language of the black church: the suffering servant, a grace-centered piety, a concern with human fallenness, and a preoccupation with evil. In short, King gave voice to the demand for black freedom in theological as well as in political terms, with his most powerful weapon being the invocation of love. As he wrote in his book *Strength to Love* (1963): "Returning hate for hate multiplies hate, adding deeper darkness to a night already devoid of stars. Darkness cannot drive out darkness; only light can do that. Hate cannot drive out hate, only love can do that."

King also urged African Americans to embrace the philosophy of nonviolence, a position indebted to his reading of the life of Jesus and to Gandhi's philosophy of *Satyagraha*, roughly translated as "truth force" and a way of life rooted in love and compassion. King's turn to Gandhi was not new. As early as the 1920s, African American academics and religious figures like Benjamin Elijah Mays, Mordecai Johnson (the president of Howard University), and a few years later Howard Thurman, all had begun to connect Gandhi's nonviolent struggle in India to the struggle for black freedom in the United States. King, however, helped translate that philosophy into a mass movement in the United States.

Like Gandhi, King believed that suffering could be redemptive and that nonviolent direct action would quicken the demise of legal segregation. Suffering as redemptive transformed the sufferer *and* the oppressor. The view was based on an unconditional love regardless of worth and merit, and grounded in the confidence that God was active in history. As King urged African Americans to change this country, he believed that they would "imbue our nation with the ideals of a higher and nobler order." He argued that "[t]hrough [the servant's] suffering, knowledge of God [was spread] to the unbelieving Gentile and those unbelievers seeing that this suffering servant was innocent would be conscious of themselves and thereby be redeemed. The nation would be healed by his wounds." King enacted this political theology until the day he was murdered—April 4, 1968.

The influence of black churches reached beyond Dr. King and other preachers involved in the movement. In Montgomery, the importance of the Women's Political Council (WPC) cannot be overstated. Dr. Mary Fair Bucks, an English professor at Alabama State University, founded the organization in 1946, and its members were primarily Baptist and Methodist black women. The WPC took as its mission "to inspire Negroes to live above mediocrity, to elevate their thinking, to fight juvenile and adult delinquency, [and] to register and vote." This organization was by far the most civically engaged group in Montgomery up until Rosa Parks's refusal to relinquish her bus seat on December 1, 1955. The members of the council, under the leadership of JoAnn Robinson, played critical roles in organizing the Montgomery bus boycott, from preparing leaflets to spreading information to the members of the community about the form and purpose of the boycott itself. Their work, and the organization itself, reflected an extensive organizing tradition among black women (as well as deep class divisions among black women in Montgomery; Rosa Parks, for instance, was a seamstress and thus not a member of the organization of black professional women). Of course, the leadership of the Montgomery Improvement Association would be decidedly male, a reflection of the highly gendered politics of black churches and the black community in general.

Just as black women struggled for leadership positions in churches, just as they were denied ordination in most mainline black denominations, black women confronted within the movement sexist assumptions about their role and place. As the efforts of the Montgomery Women's Political Council illustrate, black women organized and mobilized communities in the fight against segregation. But all too often male ministers stood in as representative figures of the movement itself. Dr. King, for example, joined with other ministers in 1957 to form the Southern Christian Leadership Conference (SCLC). No women—neither Rosa Parks nor JoAnn Robinson nor any other woman who had worked fearlessly in the Montgomery bus boycott was invited to join the organization's board. The organization quickly became one of the most important forces in the movement and represented in some ways "the decentralized arm of the black church." But those persons who helped organize SCLC, Ella Baker among them, point to a different mode of black church influence.

Ella Baker, the organization's first executive director, insisted on organizing in such a way that decentered the charismatic role of the leader. Baker's work with SCLC revealed King's own sexist commitments as he often overlooked her years of organizing experience (she worked as a field secretary for NAACP from 1940 to 1946 and as the national director of branches) and rarely treated her as an intellectual peer. As Baker wrote later, "After all, who was I? I was female, I was old. I didn't have any Ph.D."

Baker and the ministers of SCLC often clashed over their different views of leadership. She was more interested in cultivating the capacities of ordinary African Americans for democracy than in urging them to follow an anointed leader. Her approach reflected the gender dynamics of black churches, where men often assumed leadership roles in pulpits while women in the pews conducted the business of the church. Baker maintained:

> My basic sense of it has always been to get people to understand that in the long run they themselves are the only protection they have against violence or injustice…. People have to be made to understand that they cannot look for salvation anywhere but to themselves.

Her influence can be seen in her organizing efforts for the NAACP (1938–53), her role as executive director of SCLC (1957–60), and her unflinching support for the Student Non-violent Coordinating Committee (1960–66).

What is unmistakable, in each instance, was the fact that her public organizing was deeply shaped by her formative experiences in a black Baptist church in Littleton, North Carolina. Her mother, Anna Ross Baker, was actively involved in the black Baptist women's convention in North Carolina and devoutly believed in a faith enacted in good works. From a young age, Baker found herself immersed in the missionary work of activist black Baptist women, and those experiences shaped her approach to leadership. Ministers sought to lead or shepherd flocks, she maintained. Missionaries were engaged in a much more democratic practice in their efforts to gather people together, and this approach modeled her public work until she died on December 13, 1986.

To say that black churches were central to the modern civil rights movement is not to suggest that all black churches or African American Christians supported the movement. Many sat on the sidelines as others risked their lives and their sanctuaries. King, for example, found himself engaged in a memorable struggle with J. H. Jackson, the powerful preacher who led the largest black Christian organization in the country, the National Baptist Convention, USA. A veteran of Chicago machine politics, Jackson preferred the legalistic approach of the NAACP to King's call for direct action. Efforts to oust Jackson and to leverage the extraordinary power of the convention for the movement failed and, in 1961, the Progressive Baptist Convention was founded, which held civil rights and social justice as central parts of its platform.

But perhaps more important than the internal differences between black Christians about the direction of the movement were the clear differences between African American Christianity and white Christianity. King took up this challenge directly in his powerful "Letter from a Birmingham Jail" to white clergy. He and other local activists had been engaged in an extraordinary struggle in Birmingham, one of the most racially violent of southern cities. King had been jailed, and some questioned the motivations of the movement. But what disturbed him most was an article in the *Birmingham News* headlined "White Clergymen Urge Local Negroes to Withdraw Demonstrations." Among other claims, the clergy invoked religious reasons for their opposition to civil disobedience. King felt compelled to respond, and in so doing differentiated black and white Christianity. He wrote:

In deep disappointment I have wept over the laxity of the church. But be assured that my tears have been tears of love. Yes, I love the church.... Yes, I see the church as the body of Christ. But, oh! How we have blemished and scarred that body through social neglect and through fear of being nonconformists.... So often the contemporary church is a weak, ineffectual voice with an uncertain sound. So often it is an arch-defender of the status quo. Far from being disturbed by the presence of the church, the power structure of the average community is consoled by the church's silent—and often even vocal—sanction of things as they are.

Just as white missionaries and white slaveholders reconciled their commitments to Christianity with the peculiar institution, King noted that many white Christians had come to terms with the evils of Jim Crow. White Christianity did not call them to bear witness to the power of the Gospel for black people. It merely reinforced the order of things. In this historic document, King exposed the crucial difference between white Christianity and black Christianity.

Some black theologians took King's insight a step farther. The optimism of the first phase of the civil rights movement waned, and white resistance escalated in the form of white backlash. Many African Americans, some veterans of King's nonviolent approach, became increasingly skeptical about the possibility of genuine freedom in this country. Legislative victories ended legal segregation, but the real and material divides that kept African Americans languishing in poverty still obtained. Some cried out for a new mode of engagement: African Americans had to take control of the politics and economics of their own communities; they needed to learn about their history and cultural past. Proponents of this view put aside the rhetoric of love and demanded Black Power.

On July 31, 1966, an ad hoc group called the National Committee of Negro Churchmen published in the *New York Times* a statement supporting and clarifying black power in Christian terms. The statement boldly declared:

As black men who were long ago forced out of the white church
to create and to wield "black power," we fail to understand the
emotional quality of the outcry of some clergy against the use of the
term today. It is not enough to answer that "integration" is the
solution. For it is precisely the nature of the operation of power
under some forms of integration which is being challenged.... We
regard as sheer hypocrisy or as a blind and dangerous illusion the
view that opposes love to power. Love should be a controlling
element in power, but what love opposes is precisely the misuse and
abuse of power, not power itself. So long as white churchmen
continue to moralize and misinterpret Christian love, so long will
justice continue to be subverted in this land.

In some ways, the statement boldly announced a new phase of
radicalism within black Christendom. In the late 1960s, black
Christians once again sought to separate themselves from white
Christians. In 1967, for example, black delegates to the urban
conference of the National Council of Churches insisted on a
separate caucus for blacks and whites. Black Catholics organized
several all-black organizations within the Roman Catholic Church.
And in 1969 a *Black Manifesto* was issued to all white Christians.

The *Manifesto* called for reparations in the sum of $500 million
dollars to be paid by white Protestant and Catholic churches and
Jewish synagogues for their complicity in the ongoing oppression
of African Americans. It was an explicit indictment of the racial
divide at the heart of American religious life, all of which
culminated in the dramatic act by James Forman, the former
executive director of SNCC. On May 4, 1969, Forman with staff in
hand as if he were Moses going before Pharaoh walked down the
aisle of the Riverside Church in New York during Sunday service.
He literally hurled a list of demands at the minister and
congregation. This act was repeated in churches throughout the
country. A more radical expression of black Christianity had now
taken hold. The "black church" had supplanted the "negro church"
of old.

Perhaps the most sophisticated articulation of this shift was seen in the work of the prominent black liberation theologian James Cone, a professor at Union Theological Seminary. In 1969 Cone published a searing indictment of white Christianity in his first book, *Black Theology and Black Power*. Cone not only demonstrated the sheer hypocrisy of the white church, he sought to translate the prophetic black church into the idiom of black power.

It was clear that many proponents of Black Power leveled a devastating criticism of black churches and claimed new pieties or forms of religious expression as more authentically black. Some such as Walter Eugene King, who changed his name to Nana Oseijeman Adefunmi, founded separate religious communities centered on the practice of Yoruba traditions. Others like Ron Everett, who changed his name to Mualana Karenga, engaged in a creative synthesis of various African traditions in a quest to reclaim a more authentic African identity. It is in this context that the African American holiday, Kwanzaa (a holiday aimed at cultivating principles of living believed to be more consistent with the aspiration of freedom than black Christianity), was created. But Cone insisted on the continued relevance of African American Christianity to the black freedom struggle. He argued passionately that God identified with the oppressed and that the teachings of Jesus constituted a revolutionary example for those who resided on the underbelly of societies.

Cone's arguments were and remain a source of debate. Some, like his brother Cecil, a theologian in his own right, argued that he was too beholden to white theological sources. Others claimed that black liberation theology gave scant attention to the non-Christian dimensions of black religious life. Still others deftly criticized the gendered dimensions of his account: that little to no attention was given to the presence of black women's voices, their actions, and theological innovativeness. The 1970s witnessed a renaissance of black women writers and thinkers, many of whom explored spiritual themes along with questions of gender and sexuality in their work. Likewise, theologians such as Jacquelyn Grant developed what came to be known as womanist theologies, which simultaneously challenged the male-centered theology of Cone as well as presented a frontal assault on the blind spots within white feminisms. Delores Williams later defined womanist theology as "a theology of the Spirit informed by Black women's history, culture, and religious experience." Embracing those experiences and thinking about their theological significance liberate black Christianity in particular—and Christianity in general—from the double bind of racism and sexism.

Womanist theologies, Cone's black liberation theology, and the centrality of black Christianity to the civil rights movement demonstrate how the social and political circumstances of black life shaped the form and content of black Christian expression in the United States. From the Emancipation Proclamation to the election of Ronald Reagan as president of the United States, African Americans engaged in the daunting task of forging a Christian life amid the ever-shifting context of the United States. They made their way into cities in search of a Promised Land. They fought to defend democracy and freedom abroad only to be denied that freedom at home. They marched and gave expression to a complex faith that challenged the nation to live up to the true meaning of its creed. Many did so, because of the fervent belief that God was on their side. They did so proudly as *black* Christians.

Chapter 6

African American Christianity since 1980

The black freedom struggle of the 1960s and 1970s stood as a high moment in the history of black Christendom. African American Christians alongside their fellows who did not believe in God or who were members of different religious traditions successfully stared down the violence of the segregationist South and broke the back of Jim Crow. They joined with others to protest the Vietnam War, and some linked arms with those who fought for gay and women's rights. But the uncertainty of the times remained. Although legal segregation was no more, only a small percentage of African Americans experienced a fundamental shift in their quality of life.

The shift was significant. Access to elite colleges and universities (African American enrollment in colleges and universities quadrupled during this period) as well as jobs in the public and private sector, made possible by government policies such as affirmative action, resulted in an expansion of the black middle class. In the 1960s, for example, the black middle class doubled in size to 28.6 percent. By the early 1980s, that number grew to more than 37 percent. As a result of this new economic prosperity and the end of legal segregation, many middle-class black families left the inner city, and by 1986 some 7.1 million would reside in the suburbs. This rapid suburbanization dramatically impacted African American Christian life as some churches, once the cornerstone of communities in the ghetto, packed up and followed the black middle class to the suburbs.

Left behind were communities in deep crisis. The reality for the vast majority of African Americans was that too many languished in slums in America's cities; housing segregation, chronic unemployment, health disparities, rapidly rising rates of incarceration, and poor schools throughout the country ensured that no matter the legal gains of the civil rights movement, a certain segment of black America remained in the shadows. So much so that by 1979, social scientists such as William Julius Wilson warned of a permanent black underclass. Combined with staggering economic stagnation, the devastating consequences of the deindustrialization of cities as manufacturing jobs disappeared, a growing drug economy, and a widespread anti-black backlash (white anger around school busing and affirmative action), a new phase of African American Christianity began—one indelibly shaped by a national context in which a retreat from racial matters called its very existence into question.

Ronald Reagan and the Christian Right

Ronald Reagan's election in 1980 represented, for most African Americans, a retreat on racial matters. His attack on affirmative action, his calls for constructive engagement with the apartheid regime of South Africa, his eventual evisceration of the Equal Employment Opportunity Commission (EEOC) and the U.S. Commission on Civil Rights, all in the name of color blindness, signaled a change in the tone and substance of racial politics in the country. Calls for law and order, demands for smaller government, and personal responsibility became part of an arsenal of code words for white resentment and racial retrenchment.

Reagan's ascendance also facilitated the national emergence of the new Christian Right. Here a coalition of predominantly white evangelicals, led by the Reverend Jerry Falwell, a Baptist minister from Lynchburg, Virginia, aligned their understanding of the Gospel with conservative politicians who sought to "take back" the country from liberals, labor, and black folk. That coalition took the form, in the early 1980s, of the Moral Majority. After its demise in 1989, the Christian Coalition, with Pat Robertson as its leader, emerged as one of the more powerful groups. These Christians opposed affirmative action, the Equal Rights Amendment, *Roe v. Wade* (and reproductive rights generally), and a host of other liberal programs that ensured a safety net for the most vulnerable. They found a stalwart ally in Reagan himself. For many African Americans, this alliance only demonstrated, once again, the easy relationship between white Christianity and white supremacy.

Efforts to roll back the civil rights agenda (and what has been derisively called "the welfare state") occurred in the context of a broader cultural war, as conservatives extolled the virtues of Western civilization and derided claims about multiculturalism and diversity. Many worried that "the sixties" unleashed cultural patterns that threatened the moral fabric of the nation. Gun-toting black militants, bra-burning feminists, and marriage-flouting homosexuals undermined those values that made America great. What was needed was a return to tradition, narrowly conceived, where women and black folk knew their place, and the young aspired to middle-class respectability. Appeals to law and order that exercised much of the Nixon years and the rhetoric of the 1970s, driven principally by urban unrest and youthful rebellion, shaded into a much larger claim about the moral standing of the nation and its need for redemption.

These arguments played out in the American Christian community in concrete ways. The civil rights movement had forced the hand of many white Christians as they confronted collective acts of black civil disobedience. Dr. King had challenged white Christians in his April 1963 "Letter from a Birmingham Jail." And, in some ways, the choices white Christians made with regard to the black freedom struggle reimagined the lines between liberal and conservative Christians. Those who sided with efforts to broaden American democracy were liberal and represented a "new breed" of Christian. Those who did not were seen—and understood themselves—as conservative. By the end of the twentieth century, this divide between Left- and Right-leaning Christians would become as important, if not more so, than traditional denominational differences.

The transformations in American Christianity were not driven solely by politics. The emergence of charismatic preachers and their use of radio and television dramatically affected the general perception of Christianity in the United States. Evangelical broadcasters like Billy Graham and Oral Roberts and, later, the likes of Jimmy Swaggart and Jim Bakker used media to proselytize and, indeed, for individual economic gain. The history of religious broadcasters extended back to the late nineteenth and early twentieth centuries as conservative evangelicals fully embraced new technologies as part of a broader dynamic of urban revivalism (and even farther back with the revivalism of the Second Great Awakening).

Religious broadcasting did not exclude African American Christians. From religious race records that recorded the sounds of "Sanctified religion"—the Holiness-Pentecostal sounds of the urban landscape—to the recordings of such sermons as Rev. Calvin P. Dixon's 1925 "As an Eagle Stirreth Up Her Nest" or Rev. J. C. Burnett's sermon "The Downfall of Nebuchadnezzar" with women from his congregation "lining" the hymn "I heard the Voice of Jesus Say," African American Christianity was indelibly shaped by various media during the early part of the twentieth century. In 1926 Burnett's sermon outsold Bessie Smith, the legendary blues singer. Religious broadcasting would become a pronounced feature of African American Christianity in its contemporary phase.

White conservative Christians mobilized their massive media presence and their influential networks across the country in order to influence the political and spiritual direction of the country. In their hands and those of secular conservatives the sins of our racial past gave way to an emphasis on individual merit and responsibility. Persistent racial inequality was not the result of racist policies or actual discrimination. Instead, racial inequality reflected a culture of pathology, which produced bad, or minimally irresponsible people. The country, the argument went, needed to jettison the language of race altogether. We were or aspired to be a color-blind nation.

But race was everywhere in the 1980s and 1990s. Due to Ronald Reagan's pejorative use of "welfare queen" in his 1976 presidential campaign to describe a black woman on the Southside of Chicago, gaming the system had become a commonplace stereotype. The image of Willie Horton, the African American convicted of murder who in 1986 benefited from the weekend furlough program in Massachusetts only to commit armed robbery and rape, harpooned the presidential candidacy of Michael Dukakis. His image reinforced the idea of the black super-predator in the American public imagination and helped fuel the rush to mass incarceration of black and brown Americans.

Both images stood alongside events like the 1980 Miami riot in Liberty City; here, black residents turned over cars, set fire to buildings, and challenged local police and National Guardsmen because an all-white jury acquitted Miami-Dade police officers of beating to death Arthur McDuffe, a thirty-three year-old black insurance executive. Or, in the Bensonhurst section of Brooklyn, New York, in 1989, a predominantly working-class, Italian-American neighborhood, up to thirty young whites brutally attacked Yusef Hawkins, a sixteen-year-old black man and his three friends. Hawkins was shot in the chest and killed. In the 1990s, video footage of the beating of Rodney King by Los Angeles police officers transfixed the nation. After the officers were acquitted, south-central Los Angeles exploded. And the trial of O. J. Simpson for the murder of his estranged white wife, Nicole Simpson, ignited racial animosities as white anger and black joy over his acquittal illustrated the clear racial divide throughout the country. As many embraced the language of color blindness, what was all too clear in the outbursts of riots and racial violence or in the persistence of racial inequality was a willful ignorance about the realities of racism that continued to haunt the nation.

African American Christianity and megachurches

African American Christians and their churches did not sit on the sidelines as the Reagan revolution and the ideology of color blindness took hold of the nation. Local churches and ministers throughout the country continued to address the pressing issues facing their congregants and the community at large. Black liberation theologians built alliances with theologians in South Africa to resist the apartheid regime as others led demonstrations for complete divestment. Jesse Jackson sought to rekindle the energies of the black freedom movement with his extraordinary run for president in 1984 and in 1988. His first campaign drew on those informal networks and pathways that aided the organizational efforts of the movement, and the campaign capitalized on the energies of black churches. Sanctuaries continued to serve as organizing sites. Churches provided financial as well as human resources to the campaign as they worked diligently to challenge the rightward swing of the Democratic Party. And Jackson captured the imagination of a cross section of the American public, winning eleven primaries and four caucuses with his sermonic style and "Rainbow Coalition" vision.

Of course, black Christians still struggled over issues of gender equality (especially in the pulpit), with class differences, and with the issue of sexuality. Black women theologians put forward an agenda that centered the experiences of African American women. Drawing on interlocking systems of oppression—gender, race, and class—these theologians challenged patriarchy in black churches and in the community at large. They resisted the masculinist language of black power and criticized the racism of white feminists.

In addition, more black women expressed interest in ministry. The 1980s saw a dramatic increase in the number of black women entering seminary or divinity schools. By 2000, the AME Church installed its first African American bishop, Vashti McKenzie. Despite the increased presence of black women in the ministry and in positions of leadership within churches, women still face rampant sexism within black congregations. Efforts to respond to sexism also joined with attempts to push black churches toward a more progressive stance on questions of sexuality and on the epidemic of HIV/AIDS in black communities. Both revealed that when we control for issues of race, African American Christians turn out to be among the most conservative Christians on so-called "values questions" in the country.

Even with these internal contradictions, many black churches remained on the frontlines in confronting the rising tide of social misery in black America. Ministries like those of Johnny Youngblood at St. Paul Community Baptist Church in East New York, Jeremiah Wright of Trinity United Church of Christ in Chicago, and J. Alfred Smith Sr. of Allen Temple Baptist Church in Oakland, California, carried on the tradition of the institutional church and prophetic preaching of the social gospel as they engaged in social service delivery in devastated communities. They did so bearing the markings of a church transformed by the black freedom struggle. Each, in varying ways, embraced an Afrocentric expression of Christianity. The motto of Trinity United Church of Christ, for example, is "Unashamedly Black and Unapologetically Christian."

For churches like these and for those who did not espouse black liberation theology, it became increasingly clear that as conservative forces eroded the social safety net and shrank the size of government, they would have to step into the breach to provide for the most vulnerable in African American communities. In some cases, African American churches collaborated with government in faith-based poverty relief programs. Many churches found themselves involved in economic ventures within communities such as funding housing projects, establishing credit unions, offering job training and the like. In short, the politics of black churches extended beyond protest marches or mobilizing black voters.

These efforts were caught up in broader processes that transformed the nature of black public life in particular and American public life in general. The economic philosophy of neoliberalism not only involved a rethinking of the role of the state—the state was to be merely the guarantor of the proper functioning of markets and to provide for our national defense—it also resulted in a particular idea of who we take ourselves to be as Americans. Neoliberalism narrowed the idea of citizen. Any concept of the public good or responsibility for our fellows (those at the heart of Dr. King's notion of the Beloved Community) was displaced by the idea that human beings ought to engage in the rational pursuit of self-interest. A robust idea of citizenship gave way to a crude notion that Americans are simply individual entrepreneurs and consumers.

This economic philosophy undergirded the outright attack on the successes of the civil rights movement. So much so that neoliberalism helped usher in a new regime of race in the country: where the idea of the state's role as a guarantor of equality was no longer viable, personal responsibility was the single most important explanation for persistent inequality, and the idea of color blindness trumped any appeal to race (even as a few black and brown faces ascended to heights unimaginable in the previous decades). This view shaped the national political landscape from Reagan through the Clinton years and continues to inform the way we address race even with the nation's first African American president, Barack Obama.

In so many ways, the contemporary phase of African American Christianity stands as the culmination of the dramatic forces unleashed at the dawn of the twentieth century—forces that transformed black America and the nation as a whole. The consolidation of Jim Crow in the South, the massive movement of black populations into cities, the significance of World War II, and the struggle for black freedom that eventually ended legal segregation joined with new technological advances that transformed the lives of every American, the ascendance of the United States as a global power, broader movements to expand the idea of democracy in the country, the transformations within American Christianity, and the reorganization of race under the banner of color blindness. African American Christianity could not help but be transformed in the face of the torrid forces of the last century.

But those transformations were not simply the result of external events that pressed in on black Christians. Internal shifts within black Christendom reconfigured the contours of African American Christian expression as the influence of "neo-Pentecostalism" blurred denominational lines or ignored them altogether. Moreover, the changing economic and racial landscape—the emergence of a new black middle class and the ascendance of the Age of Reagan—changed the form and content of the black institutional church as it morphed, in some cases, into a new phenomenon called the megachurch.

One of the remarkable features of contemporary African American Christianity is the ascendance of Pentecostalism. By the 1960s, this once marginal religious tradition, often considered the spiritual purview of the poor and working poor, reached a worldwide membership of nearly 8 million people. Its effusive style of worship (dynamic preaching, speaking in tongues, and an overall expressivist praise), which had already influenced modern gospel music, now influenced the worship services of mainline black denominations.

Neo-Pentecostalism refers to the embrace of the particular style of worship that defines Pentecostalism without a strict adherence to its doctrine. A preacher or church could remain within the ecclesial structure, say, of the AME Church, but "worship and praise" in a way that looked and sounded like Pentecostalism. In their exhaustive study of black churches, C. Eric Lincoln and Lawrence Mamiya identified Bishop John Bryant, the former pastor of the Bethel AME Church in Baltimore, as an example of the wonderful adaptive dynamism of some mainline black churches. Bryant took a church with about five hundred members in the mid-1970s and, within ten years, pastored a congregation of over six thousand. He emphasized "a deeper spirituality." He held "informal, less structured and highly spirited worship services" that attracted students who were away from home and who often identified as Holiness or Pentecostal.

In some ways, neo-Pentecostalism stands as an example of religious bricolage. As mainline black denominations faced changing demographics as the new black middle class rushed to the suburbs, and as they confronted a more competitive religious marketplace with the "mainstreaming" of Pentecostalism, many black preachers and churches adapted to their new environments and adopted a Pentecostalized spirituality as a means to revitalize their church spaces. Pastor Frank Reid, the minister who succeeded Bishop Bryant at Bethel AME, went as far as to say that every Christian "must have a Pentecostal experience."

Bishop Paul Morton, founder of the Full Gospel Baptist Church Fellowship, illustrates the scope and influence of neo-Pentecostalism. One already notices the shift. Morton is a *Baptist* bishop, an odd description, given the congregational organization of Baptists. But Morton broke away from the National Baptist Convention in 1993 as he sought to develop a fellowship of Baptist churches committed to operating in the fullness of the Holy Spirit. His is a fellowship of Baptists linked by their embrace of a neo-Pentecostal style of worship.

To be clear, neo-Pentecostalism does not describe a theological orientation. It accounts for a mode of expression touched by classical Pentecostalism without strict adherence to doctrine. The unmooring from doctrine works in two directions simultaneously: it breaks loose from the strictures of classical Pentecostalism, and it disrupts the "stuffiness" of mainline black denominations. People are shouting in praise. Some are speaking in tongues. And they are doing this in Methodist, Baptist, Episcopal, and in Catholic churches. This form of praise has resulted in more fluid boundaries between denominations but not in their complete elimination. In some cases, churches organize outside of denominational structures all together. They often refer to themselves as nondenominational or interdenominational, and prefer to organize themselves into loose networks of affiliated congregations. But neo-Pentecostalism does not herald a postdenominational age; instead, it powerfully illustrates the creative and adaptive capacity of African American Christianity.

It is in this context that another distinctive feature of the contemporary landscape of black Christendom emerged: the ascendance of the "megachurch" and the "celebrity preacher." Megachurches are those churches with two thousand or more members. They are complex businesses with diversified portfolios. Celebrity preachers are typically the pastors of these institutions with a national and international reach across a wide range of media platforms (print, television, radio, and Internet). Their churches stand among the fastest growing sectors of black Christianity and do not easily fit within a story of African American Christianity that marginalizes Pentecostalism.

Their sanctuaries often do not have the cross as a centerpiece; instead, they appear as stages for an eventful production.

Worship services stand as a complex cross between Bible study and "Pentecostalized" praise. One walks into a sanctuary and immediately notices big screens that project live footage of the service periodically with biblical verses or words to the hymns or gospel songs. Praise is intricate as dancers and ministers of music lead the congregation in extended worship. Folks sing. They lift their hands in praise of God. Tears flow. The spirit overtakes and some get "happy"—they feel the in-flowing of the Holy Spirit and are possessed by its power. Often with a choreographed dance, the experience is heightened. During the sermon, lights dim and cameras pan in and out as the production of the "event" crescendos with the pastor's climatic end. This is theater at its best.

8. The "megachurch" is a distinctive feature of contemporary African American Christianity. Worship services entail elaborate stage productions, displayed on large screens throughout the sanctuary and broadcast across a range of media platforms including the Internet and television.

Even the demographic profiles of megachurches are markedly different. They are principally located in Sunbelt cities like Los Angeles, Houston, Atlanta, and Dallas (in some ways, they reflect the reversal of the Great Migration as African Americans began to move back to the South). Most of the churches achieved megachurch status after 1980. They are relatively young ministries with relatively young parishioners who are disproportionately middle class. Also, their size typically dwarfs traditional black churches. As such, the scope and reach of their ministries greatly advanced traditional means of church outreach.

So the demographics are changing, and this is taking place at a moment when most traditional, mainline black churches have experienced little growth. The rapid suburbanization of the black middle class affected the spatial location of many black churches as the institution followed their trail. As such, the neighborhood church and its connection to black communal interests seem to be a relic of the past. Moreover, the newfound prosperity of the black middle class (much of which vanished after the Great Recession of 2008) and their mobility affected the religious marketplace as they sought new church experiences that aligned with their status and location.

Some pastors of megachurches are often, though not always, proponents of what is called "prosperity gospel." This view holds that God wills that those who are "born again" be materially wealthy and free of disease. Known also as the "Health and Wealth Gospel" or "Faith Message," the theology connects a wide range of nondenominational and charismatic ministries rooted in the "Word of Faith Movement" that took off in the 1980s. This movement is connected to such figures as the late Kenneth Hagin Sr. and Oral Roberts, and can be traced back to the influence of New Thought and the writing of Essek William Kenyon, founder of the Bethel Bible Institute.

The impact of prosperity preaching can be seen in the enormous congregations that espouse the theology. The Reverend Frederick

K. C. Price, founder of the Crenshaw Christian Center in Los Angeles, has more than eighteen thousand members on its rolls. Creflo Dollar of World Changers International Ministries in College Park, Georgia, boasts more than thirty thousand members, and there are a host of other such institutions. The influence of prosperity gospel also reaches beyond those churches and pastors who directly espouse word of faith. Because of the scope and reach of televangelism and today's media-driven religious marketplace, aspects of prosperity gospel can be found throughout black Christendom. One can hear versions of prosperity in the charismatic ministry of T. D. Jakes of Potters House and in the progressive ministry of Freddie Haynes of The Friendship-West Baptist Church, both of Dallas, Texas, when they preach that financial success can be seen as the reward for being a faithful child of God.

One fascinating aspect of the ascendance of megachurches and celebrity pastors with their gospel of wealth is its convergence with the economic philosophy of neoliberalism and the regime of color-blind racism. Prosperity gospel blunts criticism of structures of racial inequality. It short-circuits mobilization around resource-deprived communities, precisely because wealth and the aspiration for upward mobility are tied to individual spiritual considerations. Wealth and poverty constitute evidence of God's blessings or punishment. This view of poverty adds sacred authority to cultural pathology arguments: that the poor are poor because of their bad spiritual choices. What results from this particular theology is a kind of disentangling of African American Christianity from political concerns, which enables an understanding of the black Christian as a "blessed entrepreneur and consumer." Here aspirations for freedom get lodged in claims about economic independence that all too easily align with conservatism, and the sense of African American Christianity as a response to the racial regime of the day gets cast aside. The phenomenon may even suggest that we have entered a post–black Christian moment, where the phrase "African American

Christianity" no longer singles out anything other than the fact of African Americans who are Christian. The political backdrop of African American religion is muted here as the cultural version of African American Christianity is expressed in "Pentecostalized praise."

Of course, much more has to be studied about these churches and their political significance before we pronounce something as post–black Christian. Black megachurches are significantly involved in political issues and community development. Based on a survey of more than fifty black megachurches, 96 percent are involved in voter registration drives, over 60 percent advocate on behalf of particular ballot issues, 73 percent report being directly involved in issues around Affirmative Action, and 60 percent around women's rights/empowerment. This political activity stands alongside community development initiatives with 95 percent of black megachurches reporting some substantive engagement with business activity (ranging from child-care centers to church bookstores). Sixty one percent indicate they have helped in job referral and job training; 56 percent indicate they have formed some kind of community development corporation.

The point here is not so much to demonstrate that black megachurches and their charismatic leaders are akin to traditional black churches in their political orientations. Instead, what is required is a more sustained analysis of the significance of this iteration of African American Christianity and its relation to the ideology of color blindness. Black megachurches and their preachers reveal the dynamism at the heart of African American Christianity. That dynamism can be seen not only in megachurches, in neo-Pentecostal styles of worship among large churches that are part of mainline denominations, but also in the complex ways African American Christianity negotiates late modern capitalism (through media and popular forms like contemporary gospel/praise and worship, and even hip-hop culture).

To suggest that perhaps the moment is best described as a post–black Christian one is not to disparage the current state of affairs. It releases our understanding of African Americans who are Christian from the often burdensome view that their faith must necessarily be political in some particular way. During the 2008 Democratic primary, narrow descriptions of African American Christianity produced profound misunderstandings among fellow citizens. Jeremiah Wright's fiery sermons shocked many white Americans and confirmed for others the prophetic function of the black church. Even Rev. Wright, in defending himself against the wholesale onslaught against his lifelong ministry, took himself to be defending *the* black church against crude caricature. Yet and still, his defense failed to capture the vitality and vibrancy of black Christian life: many African American Christians, in fact, reject *his* Afrocentric liberation theology, and many of them do attend megachurches and do not embrace an African American social gospel.

In the end, significant demographic and political shifts have changed the face of contemporary African American Christianity. The neighborhood church is fast disappearing. More and more African Americans are joining large megachurches and are engaged in neo-Pentecostal worship. The influence of celebrity preachers continues to grow as they leverage various media to propagate their message and their brand. All the while the political and economic circumstances of black America continue to worsen, and one wonders what role might this particular expression of African American Christianity play in the lives of so many who suffer in the shadows.

Chapter 7
African American Islam

In 1762, an African prince was born in what is now present-day Guinea. His father, Sori, was the king of Timbo and the Fulbe people, the leader of a thriving Muslim community. Sori named his son Abd Al-Rahman Ibrahima, sent him to Qur'an school, and insisted that when Ibrahima was twelve he travel to Jenna and Timbuktu to continue his studies. Ibrahima returned five years later to join his father as a learned man in Islam and to lead his armies in *jihad* against surrounding non-Muslim villages. They would eventually find themselves participating in the brutal practice of the transatlantic slave trade. A European slaver, John Ormond of Liverpool, provided the Fulbe with goods and guns, and they, in turn, provided him with gold, ivory, and slaves.

War and the slave trade yielded the Fulbe people many riches. But they also dealt King Sori a tragic blow. Ibrahima led two thousand soldiers into battle only to be ambushed and captured. His clothing and carriage revealed to his captors that he was a prince. Stripped of his clothes and shoes, Ibrahima was forced to walk one hundred miles to the Gambia River where he was sold to the Mandinka slatees (black or mulatto slave merchants), who in turn sold him to European slave traders for "two flasks of powder, a few trade muskets, eight hands of tobacco, and two bottles of rum." Ibrahima, who had once sold captured infidels into slavery, now found himself chained and bound to other condemned souls in the bowels of the slave ship *Africa*. On April 21, 1788, he was sold to Thomas Foster, a tobacco and cotton farmer in Natchez, Mississippi.

Ibrahima was one of the forty thousand or so Muslim slaves among 10 to 12 million slaves in the United States by 1860. Stories abound of slaves who prayed five times a day or who spoke a "strange tongue." In the Georgia Sea Islands a white woman named Georgia Conrad wrote of the Bilali family in the 1850s:

> On Sapelo Island near Darcen, I used to know a family of Negroes who worshipped Mohamet. They were tall and well-formed, with good features. They conversed with us in English, but in talking among themselves they used a foreign tongue that no one else understood. The head of the tribe was a very old man named Bi-la-li. He always wore a cap that resembled a Turkish fez.

Her story stands alongside countless others of slaves, like Ibrahima, who refused to forget their Muslim traditions or to abandon their religious identities. But their numbers were few.

To tell the story of Islam in America by beginning with slavery does not reveal much, beyond the important historical fact that Islam was indeed practiced among slaves. But to assert some connection between that fact and subsequent iterations of Islam in America is all too often to engage in a broader political project to think about African-descended people in the United States apart from the racist practices of white people.

None of the elements of African Islam actually shows up in the various expressions of African American Islam. Islam is embraced here under particular circumstances and in specific ways. Understanding African American Islam then is not a matter of uncovering a continuous practice of the religion. Beyond the actual presence of Muslims in the slave population, there is little to no inheritance to trace from that moment to now. Instead, we do better to think about Islam among African Americans as a feature of the rapid modernization and radicalization of black America—that period when African Americans entered cities, fought wars, experienced new forms of labor discipline, and organized formally and informally to resist white supremacy in the South and in the North. To put the point more baldly, Islam heralds "the modern" in black life.

African American Islam emerges as a religious practice in an urban, northern landscape that, at once, announces a different set of pieties and a new religious and political identity. As such, Islam among African Americans has always been a sign, a symbolic language bound up with a deep-seated suspicion of Christian practice and a healthy skepticism about the U.S. nation-state, both of which are implicated in the evils of white supremacy. Its form and content has been shaped by the startling movement of populations in the twentieth century: from those African American southerners who boldly left the brutal repression of the South only to find themselves caught within the new and distinctive challenges of northern ghettoes to those Arab and West African immigrants, after 1965, who came to the United States and claimed a more authentic and "orthodox" expression of the tradition.

The story of African American Islam, then, is not one that starts with slavery. It begins with the religious imagination of black urban dwellers in the twentieth century who deployed Islam in their efforts to forge a distinctive identity as free black men and women, and whose children would later struggle to join more fully a global Muslim community that often viewed them and the history of their unique expression of Islam with skepticism. The story of African American Islam charts that journey from the proto-Islamist movements of Noble Drew Ali and the early Nation of Islam to the efforts of the late Warith Deen Muhammad. It entails an account of the impact of what has been called immigrant Islam on the form and content of African American Islam and questions whether this expression of the Islam should be thought of as an example of African American religion.

Proto-Islam and religious bricoleurs

At the dawning of the twentieth century, one of the distinctive features of "modern" black life was its preoccupation with international matters. By the end of the nineteenth century, African American missionaries had already begun to imagine their Christian witness in global terms. They traveled to Africa and to Latin America spreading the Gospel. And many, in the face of the brutal violence of what was fast becoming the Jim Crow regime, recognized connections among the darker peoples of the world rooted in biblical prophecy. A kind of salvific history emerged as black theologians saw in Psalm 68:31—"Princes shall come out of Egypt; Ethiopia shall soon stretch out her hands unto God" (KJV)—a unique mission of African-descended people to the world. As Edward Wilmot Blyden, one of the remarkable black minds of the nineteenth century, declared in 1862, "Africa will furnish a development of civilization which the world has never yet witnessed."

The backdrop to this global, black, religiously imagined community involved fundamental shifts in the nature of capitalism and the execution of the power of states. After all, this was an era of the new imperialism, an "Age of Empire," where colonial peripheries, often imagined as the white man's burden, provided unimaginable wealth to European metropoles. The European scramble for Africa between 1881 and 1914 resulted in the startling fact that the inhabitants of Africa, almost without exception, now lived under empires, as did those who lived in the Pacific and Southeast Asian islands. The United States did not stand idly by in the face of this economic and military scramble for the raw resources of so-called backward peoples. Instead, the United States briefly took up the European model of colonialism, imagined itself as an "empire of right," and between 1898 and 1917 took hold of the Philippines, Guam, Puerto Rico, and Hawaii. And they did so at the very moment that the racial ideology of Jim Crow was consolidated in the American South.

Much of this imperial world collapsed after the two world wars. The Habsburg Empire shattered into fragments after World War I while the Ottoman Empire became a moment in world history books. The League of Nations, founded in 1919, promised a world of free states only to fail miserably in the face of the exercise of global power. Black and brown peoples found themselves moved about as pawns in the global chess games of Europe. Their quest for self-determination ran aground as white supremacy still reigned in global matters. W. E. B. Du Bois noted this fact with strident criticism in his essay "The Souls of White Folk" (1920). Du Bois described (with the betrayal of the Treaty of Versailles clearly in mind) what Europe was doing as "the doctrine of the divine right of white people to steal." Even with the convulsions of war, the ideology of white supremacy reigned. And World War II revealed the depth of that ugliness as Europe turned on itself once again—this time with the barbarity of concentration camps and their ovens. The war signaled the death of the empires of old and the end of the Age of Europe as black and brown peoples began to strike their own blows for freedom.

The embrace of Islam among African Americans must be understood against the backdrop of these global dramas. When Edward Wilmot Blyden, often considered the father of pan-Africanism, argued that African-descended people should convert to Islam in the nineteenth century, he did so because he believed the religion best fit his "civilizationist" project. Christianity had been a tool for terror and genocide, he wrote. But Islam enabled a kind of national unity among Africans. In Blyden's *Christianity, Islam, and the Negro Race* (1887), Africans "gather under the beams of the Crescent not only for religion, but for patriotic reasons; till they are not only swayed with one idea, but act as one individual. The faith becomes a part of their nationality." His was a political not a religious embrace: an insistence on the compatibility of Islam with a project of black self-determination.

Among African Americans, Islam served as a sign of difference: a way of differentiating a religious path supposedly unsullied by the nastiness of white supremacy and a geopolitical identity that enabled African Americans to see themselves as part of an imagined community beyond the borders of the United States. Just as Marcus Garvey took up the symbolic dressings of empire to give voice to an idea of black identity that embraced notions of self-determination, dynamic black personalities at the dawning of the twentieth century who embraced Islam gave voice to a religious and political identity, which radically defined black folk over and against the parochial bonds of the U.S. context. In other words, Islam-as-sign in the hands of African Americans such as Noble Drew Ali and Elijah Muhammad became a path to a kind of global blackness, which, in turn, recast its meanings within the United States. But this reimagining was not solely limited to the idea of blackness. These figures took hold of Islam as their own. They not only reconstructed the idea of blackness, they reimagined the meaning of Islam by bending and shaping it to respond to the specific conditions of black people in the United States.

In this sense, Noble Drew Ali, Elijah Muhammad, and others were indeed religious bricoleurs. They poached and picked among various religious traditions and other esoteric forms, and created something distinctively their own. The fact that they called it Islam shows how they participated in a circuit of global exchange—identifying themselves as Moors or as Asiatics in order to contest an idea of black people as born in slavery and destined for second-class status, and thus connect themselves to a broader current of religious and political meanings. Religious bricolage entails the exercise of a vibrant religious imagination, and it is here—in reaching for new ways of being in the world apart from white people and in creating new forms of religious identification—that African American Islam finds its beginnings.

Noble Drew Ali and the Moorish Science Temple

Noble Drew Ali was born Timothy Drew on January 8, 1886, in North Carolina. Not much can be said with certainty about his early days. Most accounts fit within doctrinal efforts to sacralize his beginnings (as was the case for many charismatic religious leaders of the period). His early life is shrouded in mystery and myth. It is said that at the tender age of sixteen, he joined the merchant marines and traveled to Egypt. There he met "the last priest of an ancient cult of High Magic who took him to the Pyramid of Cheops, led him in blindfolded, and abandoned him." Drew found his way out, the story goes, proving that he was a prophet, was initiated into the mysteries of the order and renamed Noble Drew Ali. Some members of the organization also believed that he traveled to Morocco and Saudi Arabia, was given permission to teach Islam in the United States, and renamed Ali by Sultan Abdul Ibn Said in Mecca. He returned to the United States in 1910, worked on the railroad, and joined the Prince Hall Masons, a branch of freemasonry for African Americans founded in the eighteenth century. No matter the truth of the stories, domestic and international travel characterized Ali's life journey. The Moorish Science Temple takes shape in the movement across these various spaces or geographies and in the context of the routes of global, even if imagined, cultural exchange.

By most accounts, Noble Drew Ali founded the Moorish Science Temple, initially called the Canaanite Temple, in 1913 in Newark, New Jersey. Ali called himself the second prophet of Islam. But from the beginning, the label of Islam worked more like a sign of difference from white Christianity than a description of actual religious practices. What distinguished members of the group was not their practice of the five pillars of Islam, but their distinctive embrace of a national identity and creed that called into question their allegiance to the U.S. nation state. Ali claimed that African Americans were not "negroes" but "Asiatics," descendants of Moroccans who "could trace their genealogy to Jesus, a descendant of "the ancient Canaanites, the Moabites, and the inhabitants of Africa." Every member of the Moorish Science Temple was given a new name and a national identity card that made explicit that their allegiances and pieties lay elsewhere. They performed that difference with their style of dress as well, as male members donned fezzes and wore "eastern-looking" clothing. Such a reorientation, along with a true knowledge of self, Ali taught, would free African Americans from the burdens of American racism.

9. Noble Drew Ali (*first row, standing, in white jacket*), in the cultural garb that he pioneered, with members of the Moorish Science Temple of America in Newark, New Jersey. Ali's proto-Islamic movement identified African Americans as descendants of Moors or Asiatics in order to challenge an idea of black people as born in slavery and destined for second-class status.

After a decade or so of preaching and organizing temples in Detroit, Pittsburgh, Chicago, Philadelphia, Richmond and Petersburg, Virginia, and Baltimore, Ali and the Moorish Science Temple boasted of a membership of about thirty thousand. Ali eventually moved the headquarters to Chicago and incorporated in 1928, renaming the organization The Moorish Science Temple of America and finally settling on the name The Moorish Divine and National Movement of North America, Inc. During this period, Ali published *The Holy Koran* or *The Circle Seven Koran*, the scripture of the organization.

But, again, this book had little, if any, connection to the Qur'an of Islam. Instead, the holy book of the Moorish Science Temple is a sixty-four-page compilation of "sacred knowledge" drawn from a number of different sources. It was as if Ali sought to cast an incantation by cobbling a vast array of esoteric knowledge that might release African Americans from their psychological and physical bondage. He drew liberally from Levi Dowling's *The Aquarian Gospel of Jesus Christ* (1920) and copied sections from the Rosicrucian book *Unto Thee I Grant* or *The Infinite Wisdom*, which claimed to be a translation of an ancient Tibetan text. Each text offered a window into what was possible if human beings would learn the true secrets of the universe (secrets unlocked by those like Drew Ali who held the keys): that liberation was in fact in our hands and that salvation rested with our doings in this world.

In the last chapter of *The Circle Seven Koran*, Ali declares himself the last prophet of Allah sent to redeem men from their sins and to warn them of the wrath to come. Marcus Garvey is figured as John the Baptist who prophesies Ali. But beyond that, the book ends with its political purpose made perfectly clear.

> Come all ye Asiatics of America and hear the truth about your nationality and birthrights, because you are not negroes. Learn of your forefathers ancient and divine Creed. That you will learn to love instead of hate.

> We are trying to uplift fallen humanity. Come and link
> yourselves with the families of nations. We honor all the
> true and divine prophets.

Islam functions here as a placeholder for an imagined community predicated on black self-determination. In doing so, and in Ali's hands, Islam becomes inextricably linked to an imagined freedom that is not bound by U.S. borders and white supremacist practices.

Most of the members of the Moorish Science Temple were working-class men and women struggling to build lives amid the torrents of the early twentieth century. Just as working-class, black, southern migrants ushered in the "Age of Voice," with blues and gospel music as the sound track of cities, these same folk transformed the religious landscape of black America by imagining new ways to give expression to their religious commitments. One heard their creations in storefront churches and in temples and mosques. This was not only an "Age of Voice," it was a time of religious ferment. Black Moors walked the streets with their distinctive fezzes alongside black Pentecostals, Garveyites, Jehovah Witnesses, and, later, bow-tied black men and fully covered women who called themselves Muslims proclaimed Fard Muhammad as Allah in the person, and believed that Elijah Muhammad was his last messenger.

Elijah Muhammad and the Nation of Islam

Born in Sandersville, Georgia, in 1897, Elijah Poole became one of the millions of African Americans who made the trek from the Jim Crow South to northern cities. In *Plessy v. Ferguson* the Supreme Court had sanctioned Jim Crow just one year earlier. And states like Georgia began to draw strict legal, social, and economic boundaries that seemingly tried to choke the life out of black folk. Jobs were limited and paid barely subsistence wages. Peonage waited in the shadows. Racial violence loomed as a constant threat, and the idea of dignity in the South for black men and women appeared to be a dangerous illusion. Poole left for Detroit in 1923 with his wife, Clara Evans (who played a critical role in the development of the Nation of Islam during Elijah Muhammad's time in jail), in search of work and a better life only to confront the misery of black urban existence during the Depression years.

Between 1890 and 1930, Detroit saw a 611 percent increase in the size of its black population. In the 1920s and 1930s, they were joined by thousands of Muslim immigrants from Turkey, Syria, Lebanon, and Albania. The collapse of the Ottoman Empire in the aftermath of World War I spurred a massive migration, many of whom were attracted to Detroit. The point here is a straightforward one: there was a Muslim presence in many northern cities in the early part of the twentieth century. They were members of the Ahmadiyya movement in Islam, a mission of Indian Ahmadis to the United States, who published the first English translation of the Qur'an in 1917. Others were members of the Islamic Mission of America headed by Shaykh Dauod Ahmed Faysal in New York in 1924, a group influenced by the teachings of the Pakistani thinker Abu al-Mawdudi and who aligned themselves with other Sunni Muslims in the world. Poole entered a religious landscape teeming with the familiar and with religious difference.

In 1930 W. D. Fard, an ambiguous figure thought to be Arab, appeared in Detroit, purportedly peddling wares. As he sold his goods he engaged his customers, teaching them that they were the "lost-found tribe of Shabazz" who had lost knowledge of their true selves. He drew on the Bible and the Qur'an as he wove a unique history of the "negro" presence in the world. As word spread about Master Fard's teachings, more and more of the working black poor of Detroit wanted to hear what he had to say. Elijah Poole met Master Fard in 1931 just as Poole felt himself spiraling downward into the depths of despair, and that meeting transformed his life. Poole believed that Fard was God incarnate, that he was the "one we read in the Bible that... would come in the last days under the name Jesus." He asked Fard if this was so, and Fard acknowledged his true divinity. Elijah Poole joined him and was renamed Elijah Muhammad.

By 1934 Fard disappeared, leaving Elijah Muhammad as the steward of the Nation of Islam (NOI). Before his disappearance, Fard had already established the Temple of Islam, a university for the teaching of doctrine, the Muslim Girls Training (MGT) class for the propagation of its views about women's proper roles, and the Fruit of Islam (FOI), the paramilitary wing of the NOI. Elijah Muhammad left Detroit for Chicago, and the mystery of Master Fard became a central part of the theology of the Nation and of Muhammad's sacred authority. He was the last messenger of Allah.

Muhammad claimed that Fard was from Mecca, Saudi Arabia—that his very presence in the United States, among black people, signaled that these "lost people" had to think of themselves in global and in religious terms. They were the original men and women of the earth, not former slaves and second-class citizens. Islam was the sign under which that distinctive identity was to be known and lived. Like Moors, members of the NOI understood themselves in terms much broader than those provided by their socialization as African Americans. Even if their interpretation of Islam barely resembled that of the majority of Muslims in the world, they understood themselves as part of a global community that reinvested blackness with sacred significance. And that view of blackness, Muhammad taught, would break the stranglehold of white supremacy around the necks of "the so-called American negro."

For Muhammad, African Americans had to be remade. This reinvention involved exposure to parts of the Christian tradition, pieces of Islam, an elaborate myth structure, and submission to a strict disciplinary code that clearly differentiated the Muslim from the rest of the world. They needed to cleanse the mind, body, and spirit of black folk. Members of the NOI were forbidden to drink

10. Elijah Muhammad addresses an assembly of African American Muslim followers in New York City in 1964. Believers were encouraged to differentiate themselves through dietary restrictions and styles of apparel that drew from traditional Islamic teachings.

alcohol, to gamble, to engage in premarital sex, or to dance. They could not eat pork or collard greens and neck bones because these were the dietary habits of slaves. Instead, members of the NOI were taught "how to eat to live." There was a particular code of dress for men and women, and every person who joined had to drop their last name and was known simply by their first name and the letter X. The X symbolized that the converted was no longer who he or she formerly was, and it signified the unqualified rejection of "the white man's" name and heritage.

Elaborate myths buttressed this display of difference. Muhammad taught that black people were the original inhabitants of the earth some 66 trillion years ago. They spoke Arabic, practiced Islam, and were ruled in a kind of paradise by twenty-four scientists. However, 6,600 years ago, an evil scientist, Yacub, engaged in genetic engineering and created white people, a race of devils, whose religion was Christianity. And for six thousand years, Allah allowed this race to rule the earth. Muhammad prophesied that the time of the "white devil" was coming to an end, beginning with the First World War in 1914, and in the final days, a "motherplane," visible only to Muhammad and the members of the NOI, would reign down bombs on every major city inaugurating the destruction of the white world and usher in a new one ruled by the original black men and women of the earth. Muhammad's beliefs about the end of the world led him to argue for complete separation from the white man's doomed world (the NOI would argue that black people should be given seven southern states as reparations for slavery) and to prohibit his followers from engaging in social or political reform movements.

This mythology upended the alleged inferiority of black people by inverting its central premise. For the NOI, all that was black was no longer a sign of evil, of mystery, and of darkness. Blackness, in Muhammad's hands, stood as a sign of all that was good. Black people were now the gods and whites were devils. As a religious bricoleur, Muhammad brilliantly used the Bible and the Qur'an as proof for his doctrine. He argued that the unique historical condition of black people in America necessitated a distinctive introduction to the doctrine of Islam. Bits and pieces of the truth were required until the requisite maturity among African Americans was achieved. The result of his efforts, along with a host of powerful personalities, was a historically unparalleled reimagining of black identity in the United States—under the sign of Islam.

Under Elijah Muhammad the NOI continued to grow, but it was not until the 1950s, with the emergence of a dynamic and zealous young minister, Malcolm X, that the NOI gained national attention and influence. Malcolm X became the national spokesperson for Elijah Muhammad, and he relentlessly proselytized on the Nation's behalf. He opened new mosques, greatly expanded its recruiting efforts, founded the newspaper

Muhammad Speaks, and extended the NOI's influence in the black freedom struggle as a powerful counter to Dr. Martin Luther King Jr. and the nonviolent civil rights movement. Malcolm X recruited Louis Eugene Walcott, a young, dynamic, West Indian calypso singer, who would later change his name to Louis Farrakhan. Malcolm X eventually left the NOI in 1965 after a dispute with its internal hierarchy over corruption, claims about adultery committed by the Elijah Muhammad, and a desire to engage more fully in the black freedom struggle of the 1960s.

After Malcolm X's departure, Louis Farrakhan was named the national representative of the Honorable Elijah Muhammad. Muhammad died in 1975 and, before his death, surprisingly named his son, Wallace Deen Muhammad, as his successor. Wallace Muhammad made substantive changes in the doctrine of the NOI. He rejected its mythology and moved the organization more closely to Sunni Islam. Confronted with these changes and a demotion, Farrakhan eventually left the NOI and, in 1981, reconstituted the organization under what is often referred to as its second dispensation.

The Nation of Islam proved to be a powerful and long-lasting institutional presence in black America. Drawing primarily from the black working class, the NOI staked out a space for black empowerment rooted in a counter-Christian tradition—one that questioned and rejected the easy alliance between Christian doctrine and white supremacy. The organization took up the politics of respectability that so animated the black middle class and insisted that, with Islam, the "rejected and despised" could be remade and saved. This new black man and woman, bow-tied and covered, vehemently resisted the world of white people. As Elijah Muhammad wrote in the last chapter of *The Message to the Black Man*:

> The Lord of the world's Finder of we the lost members of the Asiatic Black Nation for 400 years said that the slave-masters put fear in

> our Fathers when they were babies. Allah is the only one that can
> remove this fear from us, but he will not remove it from us until we
> submit to His will, not our will, and fear Him and Him alone.

For Muhammad, Islam, although a religious identity, carried with it a politics that insisted on the unconditional freedom of African Americans. That freedom required submission to the will of Allah and his last prophet, Elijah Muhammad himself.

Muhammad believed that Islam changed the relation of those who embraced his teachings to the world in which they lived. Not so much in terms of their immediate desires or their material circumstances, but in terms of their very self-understanding. For men, it offered a powerful idea of black masculinity. For women, it assured a sense of reverence and protection (experiences that should not be easily read as a willing submission to their oppression as women, even as they fought patriarchy within the organization). It is in this transformative sense as well as in the actual contributions of the Nation of Islam that Elijah Muhammad significantly contributed to the presence of Islam in black America.

African American Muslims and immigrant Islam

Wallace (or Warithuddin) Muhammad's effort to bring the NOI into alignment with Sunni Islam played a transformative role in African American Islam generally. Within months of assuming leadership of the organization in 1975, he began what can only be called a radical Sunni reformation. He rejected the claim that W. D. Fard was God in the person, insisted that members of the NOI celebrate Ramadan, that they perform *salat* or the ritual praying five times a day, rejected the central claim that white people were devils, and in June 1975 announced that whites could in fact join the NOI. Elijah Muhammad's views about the end of the world were put aside as his son urged his followers to engage the world of politics, to take up personal responsibility for their circumstances, and to embrace patriotically the United States. Wallace Muhammad even changed the name of the organization. In 1976 the NOI was renamed *The World Community of Al-Islam in the West*; in 1981 he changed the name to *American Muslim Mission* and, later, to *The American Society of Muslims*. At the time of his death in 2008, Imam Muhammad was preparing to dismantle the organization altogether.

But perhaps the most important dimension of Warithuddin Muhammad's transformation of the NOI rested with his effort to connect African American Muslims more fully with global Islam. In the past, Islam in America worked for many African Americans as primarily a sign of difference—as a way of thinking about blackness within a global context, which enabled an understanding of black people apart from American racism. Most Muslims around the world and some within the United States failed to see what was exactly Islamic about the Moorish Science Temple or the Nation of Islam. In fact, claims of Fard's divinity were considered *shirk*, the sin of idolatry. Here the particularism of Elijah Muhammad and Noble Drew Ali—that is, their effort to offer a religious response to the particular political reality of black suffering in the United States—obscured the more universal characteristic of Islam. Muslims were neither black nor white. They were Muslim.

Imam Muhammad's overtures to global Islam were often rooted in proving that African American Islam was in fact recognizable to the world of Muslims, especially to those who were now fully present in the United States. Muhammad established a relationship with Arab nations, was awarded twelve scholarships to send African American Muslims to Egyptian universities, and developed a close relationship with the U.S.-based Muslim Student Association (MSA), the organization that would eventually give way to the Islamic Society of North America in 1982. Both organizations played a critical role in establishing an institutional presence for Sunni Islam in the United States, but they also took a paternalistic stance in relation to African American Muslims: that black people needed to be instructed in a more authentic way of being Muslim (and many African American Muslims deferred to their vision). This often involved a rejection of any claims about Islam and its relation to questions of black freedom and identity.

At one point, Warithuddin Muhammad sought to identify African American Muslims with the African companion of the Prophet Muhammad, Bilal ibn Rabah, the first *muadhdhin* or prayer caller in Islam. Muhammad found in the figure of Bilal a personality that could give Islamic root to a conception of black identity. As he said of Bilal, he was "a Black Ethiopian slave who was an outstanding man in the history of Islam. He was the first muezzin of Prophet Muhammad (may peace be upon Him). He was so sincere and his heart was so pure that the Prophet Muhammad and the other leaders of Islam under him addressed him as 'Master Bilal.'" But this effort was criticized by immigrant Muslim leaders, and Muhammad eventually dropped the formulation altogether. In some ways, as this example suggests, the impact of immigrant Islam on African American Islam has been its attempted deracialization: the displacement of matters of race and politics, and a centering of concerns confronting the Muslim world (the politics of the Middle East, the Palestinian question, Israel, and the like). Universalism, in this instance, requires turning away from the particular issue of blackness and Islam. As a result, African American Muslims find themselves in a situation in which they must navigate American racism, address questions (especially since 9/11) of their allegiance to America as Muslims, and negotiate the way their particular histories as African Americans shadow the very way they live as Muslims in America.

One wonders, given this complicated picture, whether it even makes sense to think of African American Islam today as an example of African American religion. Of course, Minister Louis Farrakhan and members of the NOI continue to articulate a clear linkage between their identities as Muslim and their concern for the political state of black America. But Minister Farrakhan still battles, even as he has made significant gestures to the leaders of Sunni Islam, questions about the authenticity of his expression of Islam. The fact remains is that there are roughly 3 million African American Sunni Muslims in this country. They are affiliated with groups such as the Salafi movement, the Dar al-Islam movement, the American Society of Muslims, Jama at al-Tbligh, and Sufi groups. But how they articulate their commitment to Islam and the realities of racism in this country remains an open question.

Conclusion

African Americans are generally more religious than other groups in the United States. In a 2009 Pew Foundation study, 87 percent of African Americans described themselves as belonging to some religious group; 79 percent reported that religion is very important to the way they live their lives. Even among those black folk who reported no religious affiliation, 72 percent reported that religion plays a somewhat important role in their lives, and nearly half (46 percent) said that religion is very important. African Americans pray more than most Americans. Nine out of ten (88 percent) believe with absolute certainty that God exists, and 83 percent believe in angels and demons. So, by most measures, the Pew study reported, "African Americans stand out as the most religiously committed racial or ethnic group in the nation."

Eighty-three percent of African Americans are Christian. But this is a decidedly Protestant affair as 78 percent of African Americans report affiliation with some form of Protestantism, with the majority of African Americans (59 percent) belonging to a historically black church. Only 5 percent are Roman Catholic and 1 percent is Muslim. What can be readily seen here is that religion, and particularly Protestant Christianity, continues to animate much of African American life. And this is especially true for African American women—even as they continue to struggle with sexism within black churches. More than 84 percent of African American women say that religion is a very important component of their daily lives; 59 percent report that they attend church at least once a week. No other group of men and women exhibit comparable levels of religious observance. What Nannie Burroughs proclaimed in 1915 still holds today: "The Negro Church means the Negro woman."

But African American religion is much more than a description of how deeply religious African Americans are. The phrase helps us differentiate a particular set of religious practices from others that are invested in whiteness; it invokes a particular cultural inheritance that marks the unique journey of African Americans in the United States. African American religion says to those who will listen "pay attention to *this* as opposed to *that*"—and the distinction is rooted in the sociopolitical realities that shape the experiences of black people in this country.

None of this is static or fixed. Material conditions shift. Old ideologies die. New ones emerge. In some ways, the African American sociologist E. Franklin Frazier was right. He noted in his 1963 classic work, *The Negro Church in America*, that demographic shifts, dramatic changes in labor patterns, and class stratification within African American communities would change the role and function of black churches. The same holds today for how we understand African American religion.

Dramatic changes in the nature of work, demographic shifts that involve increased ethnic diversity within black communities, and deepening class stratification have greatly affected the ways we describe African American religion today. Many proponents of prosperity gospel preach primarily to middle-class congregations in megachurches far removed from resource-deprived neighborhoods. The idea of the "black church" has been complicated as immigration from the African continent and the Caribbean transformed certain urban *religioscapes*, connecting them to broad circuits of diasporic exchange. Nigerian Pentecostals stand alongside Haitian Catholics and Jamaican Anglicans with each insisting on the importance of their cultural inheritance in expressing their religious identities. To describe all of this as "black church" or as "African American Christianity" let alone as examples of African American religion extends the terms beyond recognition. Combined with the prevalence of the ideology of color blindness, the idea of African American religion becomes all the more ambiguous and unclear. And, perhaps, rightly so.

African American religion takes us to particular practices under specific conditions. As conditions shift and change, words and phrases that were once helpful in orienting us to certain practices often fall out of use, and new ones emerge as better descriptions. This is not to suggest that the distinctiveness of African American religious life has been lost. I still imagine a child somewhere in the United States is experiencing, like I did in that small church house on the coast of Mississippi, the fullness of African American religious life and the wonder of its theater. But the fear of loss all too often motivates us to hang on to outmoded descriptions.

How we talk about African American religion, how we account for the myriad ways in which a diverse, racialized group gives expression to their religious beliefs within institutions that constitute a kind of cultural inheritance requires a different language, especially when we are confronting something as wildly new as *The Preachers of L.A.*, a reality television show about celebrity preachers. Something has changed. Maybe this is what E. Franklin Frazier was reaching for. The issue in his much-maligned view was not so much that institutions and cultural languages created under one set of conditions faded from view as African Americans were more fully integrated into American society. Instead, new languages would have to emerge to describe and account for black religious experiences under the shifting conditions of late capitalism and the evolving status of race in the United States.

African American religious life remains a powerful site for creative imaginings in a world still organized by race. Churches, mosques, communions of all kinds offer African Americans who participate in them languages and identities that speak back to their conditions of living. What is required is a thick description of what is going on in the religious life of this diverse and complicated community. And if African American religion helps us in doing that work, then it remains useful. If it does not, if the phrase blocks the way to a fuller understanding of religion and race in the United States because it is an outmoded description, then it is time we got rid of it.

References

Chapter 1: The category of "African American religion"

W. E. B. Du Bois, "The Souls of White Folk," in *W. E .B. DuBois: Writings* (New York: Library of America, 1986), 493–505.

William Hart, *Black Religion: Malcolm X, Julius Lester, and Jan Willis* (New York: Macmillan, 2008), 1–15.

Charles Long, *Significations: Signs, Symbols, and Images in the Interpretation of Religion* (Aurora, CO: The Davis Group, 1995), 187–98.

Chapter 2: Conjure and African American religion

Ira Berlin, *Many Thousands Gone: The First Two Centuries of Slavery in North America* (Cambridge, MA: Harvard University Press, 1998), 1–14.

Yvonne Chireau, *Black Magic: Religion and the African American Conjuring Tradition* (Berkeley: University of California Press, 2003), 13.

Mark Claddis, introduction to Emile Durkheim's *The Elementary Forms of Religious Life* (New York: Oxford University Press, 2008), xxiii.

Frederick Douglass: Autobiographies (New York: The Library of America, 1994), 63, 64.

Frederick Douglass, *Narrative of the Life of Frederick Douglass: An American Slave Written by Himself* (New York: Penguin Books, 1982), 117.

Michael Gomez, *Exchanging Our Marks: The Transformation of African Identities in the Colonial and Antebellum South* (Chapel Hill: University of North Carolina Press, 1998), 1–37.

Zora Neal Hurston, *The Sanctified Church* (New York: Marlowe and Company, 1981), 19–20.

Lawrence Levine, *Black Culture and Black Consciousness: Afro-American Folk Thought from Slavery to Freedom* (New York: Oxford University Press, 1977), 71.

Russell McCutcheon, "Africa on Our Minds," in *The African Diaspora and the Study of Religion*, ed. Theodore Louis Trost, 232–33 (New York: Palgrave Macmillan, 2007).

"Narrative of Sylvia King," in *Voices from Slavery: 100 Authentic Slave Narratives*, ed. Norman R. Yetman, 201 (Mineola, NY: Dover Publications, 1970).

Daniel Pals, *Seven Theories of Religion* (New York: Oxford University Press, 1996), 16–53.

Albert Raboteau, *Slave Religion: The Invisible Institution in the Antebellum South* (New York: Oxford University Press, 1978), 92, 275–88.

"Narrative of Sylvia King," 201.

Theophus Smith, *Conjuring Culture: Biblical Formations of Black America* (New York: Oxford University Press, 1995), 19.

Chapter 3: African American Christianity: The early phase (1760–1863)

Bettye Collier-Thomas, *Jesus, Jobs and Justice: African American Women and Religion* (New York: Alfred A. Knopf, 2010), 23.

C. Eric Lincoln and Lawrence Mamiya, *The Black Church in the African American Experience* (Durham, NC: Duke University, 1990), 20–46.

Nathan Hatch, *The Democratization of Christianity* (New Haven, CT: Yale University Press, 1977), 9; Also see Gordon S. Wood, "Ideology and the Origins of Liberal America," *William and Mary Quarterly* 44 (1987): 637.

Peter Kalm, *Travels into North America*, 2nd ed. repr. in vol. 13 of *A General Collection of the Best and Most Interesting Voyages and Travels*, ed. John Pinkerton (London: Longman, Hurst, Rees and Orme, 1812). Quoted in Raboteau, *Slave Religion*, 102.

Charles Colcock Jones, *A Catechism of Scripture, Doctrine and Practice for Families and Sabbath Schools. Designed Also for the Oral Instruction of Colord Persons* (Savannah, GA: Observer Press, 1844), 127–30.

Charles Joyner, "Believer I Know: The Emergence of African American Christianity," in *African American Christianity: Essays in History*, ed. Paul Johnson, 21–22 (Berkeley: University of California Press, 1994).

Lawrence Levine, *Black Culture and Black Consciousness: Afro-American Folk Thought from Slavery to Freedom* (New York: Oxford University Press, 1977), 45, 32–33.

Albert Raboteau, *Canaan Land: A Religious History of African Americans* (New York: Oxford University Press, 2001), 19, 21.

Albert Raboteau, *A Fire in the Bones: Reflections on African American Religious History* (Boston: Beacon Press, 1995), 19; Thomas Secker, "Sermon before S.P.G." (1740/1; repr., in Frank J. Klingberg, *Anglican Humanitarianism in Colonial New York* (Philadelphia: Church Historical Association, 1940), 223.

Albert Raboteau, *Slave Religion: The Invisible Institution in the Antebellum South* (New York: Oxford University Press, 1978), 123.

Alexis de Tocqueville, *Democracy in America* (New York: Harper & Row, 1969), 342.

James Melvin Washington, *Frustrated Fellowship: The Black Baptist Quest for Social Power* (Macon, GA: Mercer University Press, 2004), 1–46.

David Wills, "The Central Themes of American Religious History: Pluralism, Puritanism and the Encounter of Black and White," in *African American Religion: Interpretative Essays in History and Culture*, ed. Timothy E. Fulop and Albert Raboteau, 7–22 (London: Routledge, 1997).

David Wills, *Christianity in the United States: A Historical Survey and Interpretation* (Notre Dame, IN: University of Notre Dame Press, 2005), 28–29.

Chapter 4: African American Christianity: The modern phase (1863–1935)

Kelly J. Baker, *Gospel According to the Klan: The KKK's Appeal to Protestant America, 1915–1930* (Lawrence: University Press of Kansas, 2011), 19, 29.

Wallace Best, *Passionately Human, No Less Divine: Religion and Culture in Black Chicago, 1915–1952* (Chicago: University of Chicago Press, 2005), 110–11.

Horace Clarence Boyer, "African American Gospel Music," in *African Americans and the Bible*, ed. Vincent Wimbush, 464–88 (New York: Continuum, 2003).

Randall Burkett, "The Baptist Church in the Years of Crisis: J. C. Austin and the Pilgrim Baptist Church, 1926–1950" in *African American Christianity: Essays in History*, ed. Paul Johnson, 135–36 (Berkeley: University of California Press, 1994).

Jay Riley Case, *An Unpredictable Gospel: American Evangelicals and World Christianity, 1812–1920* (New York: Oxford University, 2012),159–82.

Eric Foner, *Reconstruction: America's Unfinished Revolution, 1863–1877* (New York: HarperCollins, 1988), 1–34.

Evelyn Brooks Higginbotham, "Rethinking Vernacular Culture," in *The House That Race Built: Black Americans, U.S. Terrain*, ed. Wahneema Lubiano, 163, 165 (New York: Pantheon, 1997).

Evelyn Brooks Higginbotham, *Righteous Discontents: The Woman's Movement in the Black Baptist Church, 1880–1920* (Cambridge, MA: Harvard University Press, 1994), 150–84.

Elsie W. Mason, "Bishop C. H. Mason, Church of God in Christ," in *African American Religious History: Documentary Witness*, ed. Milton Sernett, 323, The C. Eric Lincoln Series on the Black Experience (Durham, NC: Duke University Press, 1999).

Nell Painter, *Exodusters: Black Migration to Kansas after Reconstruction* (New York: Alfred A. Knopf, 1977).

Orlando Patterson, *Rituals of Blood: The Consequences of Slavery in Two American Centuries* (New York: Basic Civitas Books, 1999), 169–232; Stephen Tuck, *We Ain't What We Ought to Be: The Black Freedom Struggle from Emancipation to Obama* (Cambridge, MA: Belknap Press, 2010), 97; Robin D. G. Kelley and Earl Lewis, eds., *To Make our World Anew: A History of African Americans from 1880*, 2 vols. (New York: Oxford University Press, 2000), 3–66.

Albert Raboteau, *Canaan Land: A Religious History of African Americans* (New York: Oxford University Press, 2001), 65, 82–123.

Reverdy C. Ransom, "The Institutional Church," *Christian Recorder* (March 7, 1901), 1.

Henry McNeil Turner, "Emigration to Africa," in *African American Religious History: Documentary Witness* (Durham, NC: Duke University Press, 1999), 290.

C. Vann Woodward, *The Strange Career of Jim Crow* (New York: Oxford University Press, 1974), 70.

Jonathan L. Walton, *Watch This! The Ethics and Aesthetics of Black Televangelism* (New York: New York University Press, 2009), 19–46.

Chapter 5: African American Christianity: The modern phase (1935–1980)

Clayborne Carson, "Martin Luther King Jr., and the African-American Social Gospel," in *African American Christianity: Essays in History*, ed. Paul Johnson (Berkeley: University of California Berkeley, 1994), 159–78.

Horace Cayton and St. Clair Drake, *Black Metropolis: A Study of Negro Life in a Northern City* (Chicago: University of Chicago Press, 1993), 418.

Bettye Collier-Thomas, *Jesus, Jobs, and Justice: African American Women and Religion* (New York: Alfred A. Knopf, 2010), 366–476.

James Cone, *Black Theology and Black Power* (Maryknoll, NY: Orbis, 1997), 31–61.

Quinton Dixie and Peter Eisenstadt, *Visions of a Better World: Howard Thurman's Pilgrimage to India and the Origins of African American Non-Violence* (Boston: Beacon Press, 2011), 85–116.

Jo Ann Robinson, *The Montgomery Bus Boycott and the Women Who Started It* (Knoxville: University of Tennessee Press, 1987), 23.

Martin Luther King Jr., "Letter from Birmingham City Jail (1963)," in *A Testament of Hope: The Essential Writings and Speeches of Martin Luther King, Jr.*, ed. James Melvin Washington, 289–302 (New York: HarperOne, 2003).

Gerda Lerner, "Developing Community Leadership: Ella Baker," in *Black Women in White America: A Documentary History*, ed. Gerda Lerna, (New York: Vintage Books, 1973), 347.

Aldon Morris, *Origins of the Civil Rights Movement: Black Communities Organizing for Change* (New York: Free Press, 1986), 77.

Nell Painter, *Creating Black Americans: African American History and Its Meanings: 1619 to the Present* (New York: Oxford University Press, 2007), 216.

Albert Raboteau, *Canaan Land: A Religious History of African Americans* (New York: Oxford University Press, 2001), 106–8; and *A Fire in the Bones: Reflections on African American Religious History* (Boston: Beacon Press, 1995), 103–16.

Barbara Ransby, *Ella Baker and the Black Freedom Movement: A Radical Democratic Vision* (Chapel Hill: University of North Carolina Press, 2003), 173, 189–95.

Barbara Savage, *Your Spirits Walk Beside Us: The Politics of Black Religion* (Cambridge, MA: Belknap Press, 2008), 20–67.

Jeanne Theoharis, *The Rebellious Life of Mrs. Rosa Parks* (Boston: Beacon Press, 2013), 1–17.

Gayraud Wilmore, *Black Religion and Black Radicalism: An Interpretation of the Religious History of Afro-American People* (Maryknoll, NY: Orbis, 1989), 196–97.

Chapter 6: African American Christianity since 1980

Wendy Brown, "Neo-liberalism and the End of Liberal Democracy," *Theory and Event* 7, no. 1 (2003): 4–5.

R. Drew Smith and Tamelyn Tucker-Worgs, "Megachurches: African American Churches in Social and Political Context," in *The State of Black America 2000: Blacks in the New Millennium* (New York: National Urban League, 2000), 171–95.

C. Eric Lincoln and Lawrence Mamiya, *The Black Church in the African American Experience* (Durham, NC: Duke University Press, 1990), 382–404.

Cheryl Townsend Gilkes, "Plenty Good Room: Adaptation in a Changing Black Church," *ANNALS, The American Academy of Political and Social Science* 558 (July 1998): 101–21.

Fredrick C. Harris, *Something Within: Religion in African American Activism* (New York: Oxford University Press, 2001), 177–86.

Melissa Harris-Lacewell, "Righteous Politics: The Role of the Black Church in Contemporary Politics," *Cross Currents*, June 22, 2007.

Milmon F. Harrison, *Righteous Riches: The Word of Faith Movement in Contemporary African American Religion* (New York: Oxford University Press, 2005).

Shayne Lee, *T. D. Jakes: America's New Preacher* (New York: New York University Press, 2007), 158–77.

Michael Leo Owens, *God and Government in the Ghetto: The Politics of Church-State Collaboration in Black America* (Chicago: University of Chicago Press, 2007), 1–66.

Daniel Rodgers, *The Age of Fracture* (Cambridge, MA: Harvard University Press, 2011), 128.

Jonathan Walton, *Watch This! The Ethics and Aesthetics of Black Televangelism* (New York: New York University Press, 2009), 33–35.

Sean Wilentz, *The Age of Reagan: A History, 1974–2008* (New York: Harper Perennial, 2009), 180–85.

William Julius Wilson, *The Declining Significance of Race: Blacks and Changing American Institutions* (Chicago: University of Chicago Press, 1978).

Robert Wuthnow, *The Restructuring of American Religion: Society and Faith Since World War II* (Princeton, NJ: Princeton University Press, 1988), 133–72.

Chapter 7: African American Islam

Allan Austin, *African Muslims in Antebellum America: Transatlantic Stories and Spiritual Struggles* (London: Routledge, 1997), 22.

Edward Wilmot Blyden, *Christianity, Islam, and the Negro Race* (Edinburgh: Edinburgh University Press, 1967), 228–31.

W. E. B. Du Bois, "The Souls of White Folk," in *W.E.B. DuBois: Writings* (New York: Library of America, 1986), 935.

Georgia Bryan Conrad, *Reminiscences of a Southern Woman* (Hampton, VA: Hampton Institute Press, 1900).

Edward E. Curtis IV, *Islam in Black America: Identity, Liberation, and Difference in African-American Islamic Thought* (New York: SUNY Press, 2002), 37, 48, 58–61, 69–79, 119.

Eric Hobsbawn, *On Empire: America, War, and Global Supremacy* (New York: Pantheon, 2008), 3.

Sherman Jackson, *Islam and the Blackamerican: Looking toward the Third Resurrection* (New York: Oxford University Press, 2005), 39–40, 46, 131–70.

Aminah Beverly McCloud, *African American Islam* (London: Routledge, 1995), 135–62.

Albert Raboteau, *A Fire in the Bones: Reflections on African-American Religious History* (Boston: Beacon Press, 1995), 51.

Richard Turner, *Islam in the African-American Experience* (Bloomington: Indiana University Press, 2003), 28–32, 61, 93.

Further reading

Study of religion and African American religion

Asad, Talal. *Genealogies of Religion: Disciplines and Reasons of Power in Christianity and Islam*. Baltimore, MD: Johns Hopkins University Press, 1993.

Critical Terms for Religious Studies, ed. Mark C. Taylor. Chicago: University of Chicago Press, 1998.

Evans, Curtis J. *The Burden of Black Religion*. New York: Oxford University Press, 2008.

McCutcheon, Russell. *Manufacturing Religion: The Discourse on Sui Generis Religion and the Politics of Nostalgia*. New York: Oxford University Press, 1997.

Orsi, Robert. *Between Heaven and Earth: The Religious Worlds People Make and the Scholars Who Study Them*. Princeton, NJ: Princeton University Press, 2005.

Pinn, Anthony. *Terror and Triumph: The Nature of Black Religion*. Minneapolis, MN: Fortress, 2003.

Smith, Jonathan Z. *Imagining Religion: From Babylon to Jonestown*. Chicago: University of Chicago Press, 1982.

West, Cornel. *Prophesy Deliverance! An Afro-American Revolutionary Christianity*. Louisville, KY: Westminster John Knox, 2002.

General American religious history

Abelman, Robert, and Stewart M. Hoover, eds. *Religious Television: Controversies and Conclusions*. Norwood, NJ: Ablex, 1990.

Ahlstrom, Sidney. *A Religious History of the American People*. New Haven, CT: Yale University Press, 1972.

Case, Jay Riley. *An Unpredictable Gospel: American Evangelicals and World Christianity, 1812–1920*. New York: Oxford University Press, 2012.

Gaustad, Edwin, and Leigh Schmidt. *The Religious History of America: The Heart of the American Story from Colonial Times to Today*. New York: HarperSanFrancisco, 2002.

Goetz, Rebecca Anne. *The Baptism of Early Virginia: How Christianity Created Race*. Baltimore, MD: Johns Hopkins University Press, 2012.

Luker, Ralph E. *The Social Gospel in Black and White: American Racial Reform, 1885–1912*. Chapel Hill: University of North Carolina Press, 1998.

Marsden, George. *Understanding Fundamentalism and Evangelicalism*. Grand Rapids, MI: Wm. B. Eerdmans Publishing, 1991.

Miller, Donald E. *Reinventing American Protestantism: Christianity in the New Millennium*. Berkeley: University of California Press, 1997.

Noll, Mark A. *American Evangelical Christianity: An Introduction*. Oxford: Wiley Blackwell, 2000.

Noll, Mark A., ed. *Religion and American Politics: From the Colonial Period to the 1980s*. New York: Oxford University Press, 1990.

African American religious studies

Anderson, Victor. *Beyond Ontological Blackness: An Essay on African American Religious and Cultural Criticism*. New York: Continuum, 1995.

Baer, Hans. *The Black Spiritual Movement: A Religious Response to Racism*. Knoxville: University of Tennessee, 1984.

Baer, Hans A., and Merrill Singer. *African-American Religion in the Twentieth Century: Varieties of Protest and Accommodation*. Knoxville: University of Tennessee Press, 1992.

Burkett, Randall, and Richard Newman, eds. *Black Apostles: Afro-American Clergy Confront the Twentieth Century*. Boston: G. K. Hall, 1978.

Butler, Anthea D. *Women in the Church of God in Christ: Making a Sanctified World*. Chapel Hill: University of North Carolina Press, 2007.

Cannon, Katie. *Black Womanist Ethics*. Atlanta: Scholars Press, 1988.

Chireau, Yvonne, and Nathaniel Deutsch. *Black Zion: African American Religious Encounters with Judaism*. New York: Oxford University Press, 1995.

Collier-Thomas, Bettye. *Daughters of Thunder: Black Women Preachers and Their Sermons, 1850–1979*. San Francisco: Jossey-Bass, 1988.

Curtis, Edward E. *Black Muslim Religion in the Nation of Islam, 1960–1975*. Chapel Hill: University of North Carolina Press, 2006.

Diouf, Sylviane A. *Servants of Allah: African Muslims Enslaved in the Americas*. New York: New York University Press, 1998.

Douglass, Kelly Brown. *Sexuality and the Black Church*. Maryknoll, NY: Orbis, 1999.

Fauset, Arthur Huff. *Black Gods of the Metropolis: Negro Religious Cults of the Urban North*. Philadelphia: University of Pennsylvania Press, 1970.

Frazier, E. Franklin. *The Negro Church in America*. New York: Schocken Books, 1963.

Frederick, Marla F. *Between Sundays: Black Women and Everyday Struggles of Faith*. Berkeley: University of California Press, 2003.

Frey, Sylvia, and Betty Wood. *Come Shouting to Zion: African American Protestantism in the American South and British Caribbean to 1830*. Chapel Hill: University of North Carolina Press, 1998.

Gilkes, Cheryl Townsend. *If It Wasn't for the Women*. Maryknoll, NY: Orbis, 2001.

Glaude, Eddie. *Exodus! Religion, Race and Nation in Early Nineteenth-Century Black America*. Chicago: University of Chicago Press, 1999.

Glaude, Eddie, and Cornel West, eds. *African American Religious Thought: An Anthology*. Louisville, KY: Westminster John Knox, 2003.

Gardell, Mattia. *In the Name of Elijah Muhammad: Louis Farrakhan and the Nation of Islam*. Durham, NC: Duke University Press, 1996.

Grant, Jacqueline. *White Women's Christ and Black Women's Jesus: Feminist Christology and Womanist Response*. Atlanta, GA: Scholars Press, 1989.

Harris, Michael W. *The Rise of Gospel Blues: The Music of Thomas Andrew Dorsey in the Urban Church*. New York: Oxford University Press, 1992.

Hopkins, Dwight. *Introducing Black Theology of Liberation.*
Maryknoll, NY: Orbis, 1999.

Hopkins, Dwight N., and George C. L. Cummings. *Cut Loose Your
Stammering Tongue: Black Theology in the Slave Narratives.*
Louisville, KY: Westminster John Knox, 2003.

Hucks, Tracey E. *Yoruba Traditions and African American Religious
Nationalism.* Albuquerque: University of New Mexico Press, 2012.

Johnson, Clifton H., ed. *God Struck Me Dead: Religious Conversion
Experiences and Autobiographies of Ex-Slaves.* Cleveland, OH:
Pilgrim Press, 1969.

Lincoln, C. Eric. *The Black Muslims in America.* Boston: Beacon
Press, 1961.

Maffly-Kipp, Laurie F. *Setting Down the Sacred Past: African-
American Race Histories.* Cambridge, MA: Belknap Press, 2010.

Martin, Darnise. *Beyond Christianity: African Americans in a New
Thought Church.* New York: New York University Press, 2005.

Mays, Benjamin Elijah. *The Negro's God as Reflected in His Literature.*
Boston: Chapman and Grimes, 1938.

Mays, Benjamin Elijah, and Joseph W. Nicholson. *The Negro's Church.*
New York: Institute of Social and Religious Research, 1933.

Mitchem, Stephanie. *Introducing Womanist Theology.* Maryknoll, NY:
Orbis, 2002.

Pinn, Anne, and Anthony Pinn. *Introduction to Black Church History.*
Minneapolis, MN: Augsburg Fortress, 2002.

Pitney, David Howard. *The Afro-American Jeremiad: Appeals for
Justice in America.* Philadelphia: Temple University Press,
1990.

Robeck, Jr., Cecil M. *The Azusa Street Mission and Revival.* Nashville,
TN: Thomas Nelson, 2006.

Rouse, Carolyn Moxely. *Engaged Surrender: African American Women
and Islam.* Chicago: University of California Press, 2004.

Sanders, Cheryl J. *Saints in Exile: The Holiness-Pentecostal Experience
in African American Religion and Culture.* New York: Oxford
University Press, 1996.

Sernett, Milton. *Bound for the Promised Land: African American
Religion and the Great Migration.* Durham, NC: Duke University
Press, 1997.

Sobel, Mechal. *Trabelin' On: The Slave Journey to an Afro-Baptist
Faith.* Princeton, NJ: Princeton University Press, 1979.

Thurman, Howard. *With Head and Heart: The Autobiography of
Howard Thurman.* New York: Harcourt Brace Jovanovich, 1979.

Warner, R. Stephen, and Judith G. Wittner, eds. *Gatherings in Diaspora: Religious Communities and the New Immigration.* Philadelphia: Temple University Press, 1998.

Watts, Jill. *God, Harlem, U.S.A.: The Father Divine Story.* Berkeley: University of California Press, 1992.

Weisenfeld, Judith. *African American Women and Christian Activism: New York's Black YWCA, 1905-1945.* Cambridge, MA: Harvard University Press, 1997.

Weisenfeld, Judith. *Hollywood Be Thy Name: African American Religion in American Film, 1929-1949.* Berkeley: University of California Press, 2007.

White, Calvin. *The Rise of Respectability: Race, Religion and the Church of God in Christ.* Fayetteville: University of Arkansas Press, 2012.

Williams, Delores. *Sisters in the Wilderness: The Challenge of Womanist God-Talk.* Maryknoll, NY: Orbis Books, 1993.

Woodson, Carter G. *The History of the Negro Church.* Washington, DC: Associated Publishers, 1972.

Young, Amos, and Estrelda Alexander. *Afro Pentecostalism: Black Pentecostal and Charismatic Christianity in History and Culture.* New York: New York University, 2011.

General African American history

Blight, David. *Race and Reunion: The Civil War in American Memory.* Cambridge, MA: Harvard University Press, 2001.

Branch, Taylor. *At Canaan's Edge: America in the King Years, 1965-68.* New York: Simon & Schuster, 2006.

Branch, Taylor. *Parting the Waters: America in the King Years, 1954-63.* New York: Simon & Schuster, 1988.

Branch, Taylor. *Pillar of Fire: America in the King Years, 1963-65.* New York: Simon & Schuster, 1999.

Cohen, Cathy. *The Boundaries of Blackness: AIDS and the Breakdown of Black Politics.* Chicago: University of Chicago Press, 1999.

Genevese, Eugene. *Roll, Jordan, Roll: The World the Slaves Made.* New York: Vintage, 1972.

Giddings, Paula. *When and Where I Enter: The Impact of Black Women and Sex in America.* New York: William Morrow, 1984.

Gilmore, Glenda Elizabeth. *Defying Dixie: The Radical Roots of Civil Rights, 1919-50.* New York: W. W. Norton, 2008.

Goldsby, Jacqueline. *A Spectacular Secret: Lynching in American Life and Literature.* Chicago: University of Chicago Press, 2006.

Harding, Vincent. *There Is a River: The Black Freedom Struggle in America*. New York: Vintage Books, 1993.

Jordan, Winthrop. *White Over Black: American Attitudes Toward the Negro, 1550–1812*. Chapel Hill: University of North Carolina Press, 1968.

Joseph, Peniel. *Waiting 'Til the Midnight Hour: A Narrative History of Black Power in America*. New York: Henry Holt, 2007.

Kelley, Robin D. G. *Freedom Dreams: The Black Radical Imagination*. Boston: Beacon Press, 2003.

Kelley, Robin D. G., and Earl Lewis, *To Make Our World Anew, Vol. 1: A History of African Americans to 1880*. New York: Oxford University Press, 2000.

Morgan, Jennifer. *Laboring Women: Reproduction and Gender in New World Slavery*. Philadelphia: University of Pennsylvania Press, 2004.

Payne, Charles. *I've Got the Light of Freedom: The Organizing Tradition and the Mississippi Freedom Struggle*. Berkeley: University of California Press, 2007.

Plummer, Brenda Gayle. *In Search of Power: African Americans in the Ear of Decolonization, 1956–1975*. New York: Cambridge University Press, 2013.

Reed, Adolph. *The Jesse Jackson Phenomenon: The Crisis of Purpose in Afro-American Politics*. New Haven, CT: Yale University Press, 1986.

Royster, Jacqueline, ed. *Southern Horrors and Other Writings: The Anti-Lynching Campaign of Ida B. Wells, 1892–1900*. New York: Bedford Books, 1997.

Savage, Barbara Dianne. *Broadcasting Freedom: Radio, War, and the Politics of Race, 1938–1948*. Chapel Hill: University of North Carolina Press, 1999.

Trotter, William Joe, ed. *The Great Migration in Historical Perspective: New Dimensions of Race, Class, and Gender*. Bloomington: Indiana University Press, 1991.

Van Deburg, William L. *New Day in Babylon: The Black Power Movement and American Culture, 1965–1975*. Chicago: University of Chicago Press, 1992.

White, Deborah Gray. *Ar'nt I a Woman: Female Slaves in the Plantation South*. New York: W. W. Norton, 1999.

Index

Note: Page numbers in italics refer to illustrations.